W9-BSQ-461

The Kids' Natural History Book

Making Dinos, Fossils, Mammoths & More!

BY JUDY PRESS

◆

ILLUSTRATIONS BY
MICHAEL KLINE

Williamson Publishing ◆ Charlotte, Vermont

Kids Can! ® **series editor** Susan Williamson

Project editor Emily Stetson

Illustrations Michael Kline

Design Atwater Design

Cover design Trezzo-Braren Studio

Photography page 11 (trilobite): Neg. No. 116497 Photo. Dutcher, Courtesy Dept. of Library Services, American Museum of Natural History; page 115 (Lucy bones): © John Reader, Science Source/ Photo Researchers, Inc.

Permissions Permission to use the following material is granted by Susan Williamson: pages v–ix and pages 1–18. Permission to use the following material is granted by Williamson Publishing Company: from *Ancient Greece!* by Avery Hart & Paul Mantell: page 8; *The Beast in You!* by Marc McCutcheon: pages 106, 115; *Bird Tales from Near & Far* by Susan Milord: pages 90–91; *Geology Rocks!* by Cindy Blobaum: page 77; *Great Parties for Kids* by Nancy Fyke, Lynn Nejam, Vicki Overstreet: page 82; *Kids' Art Works!* by Sandi Henry: page 119; *The Kids' Nature Book* by Susan Milord: page 49; *The Kids' Science Book* by Robert Hirschfeld & Nancy White: pages 40–41, 46, 54; *The Kids' Wildlife Book* by Warner Shedd: pages 48, 109; *Monarch Magic!* by Lynn Rosenblatt: pages 42–44; *Summer Fun!* by Susan Williamson: pages 29, 34, 36, 50.

Printing Capital City Press

LIBRARY OF CONGRESS CATALOGING-IN-PUBLICATION DATA

Press, Judy, 1944-
 The kids natural history book: making dinos, fossils, mammoths & more! /
 Judy Press.
  p. cm.
  "Williamson kids can! book."
 Includes index.
 Summary: Arts, crafts, and nature activities explore various elements of the natural world, including ocean life, insects, dinosaurs, amphibians and reptiles, birds, mammals, and early man.
 ISBN 1-885593-24-4 (alk. paper)
 1. Handicraft—Juvenile literature. 2. Natural history—Juvenile literature.
[1. Handicraft. 2. Natural history.] I. Title.
 TT160.P778 2000
 745.5 — dc21   98-30052
                                              CIP
                                              AC

WILLIAMSON PUBLISHING CO.
Box 185   Charlotte, VT 05445   (800) 234-8791

Manufactured in the United States of America

10 9 8 7 6 5 4 3 2 1

Little Hands®, *Kids Can!*®, *Tales Alive!*®, and *Kaleidoscope Kids*® are registered trademarks of Williamson Publishing Company.

Good Times™ and *Quick Starts*™ *For Kids!* are trademarks of Williamson Publishing Company.

Contents

DEDICATION

To my mother Esther Abraham, and mother-in-law, Mildred Press

Who is best taught? He who has first learned from his mother.
THE TALMUD

ACKNOWLEDGMENTS

I wish to thank the following people for their support and encouragement in the writing of this book: the Mt. Lebanon Public Library and Judy Sutton, head of children's services; Carol Baicker-Mckee; Andrea Perry; Cory Polena; Mark Polena; my husband, Allan; and my children.

This book would not have been possible without the talent and dedication of the following people at Williamson Publishing: Jack Williamson, Jennifer Ingersoll, June Roelle, Vicky Congdon, Jean Silveira, and Merietta McKenzie. A special thanks to Emily Stetson and Susan Williamson, whose perseverance propelled this book to its ultimate completion, and to designer Bonnie Atwater, illustrator Michael Kline, and cover designers Ken Braren and Loretta Trezzo-Braren, for their creativity.

YAY!

WELCOME TO THE KIDS CAN! NATURAL HISTORY MUSEUM

WELL, HERE YOU ARE. Inside a book about natural history at a place called the *KIDS CAN!* NATURAL HISTORY MUSEUM. We're aware that you don't even know if you like history — natural or not — and you aren't too sure about museums, either. So what gives?

what's a kids' Can! Museum?

Questions, questions, questions! We LOVE questions here! The more you ask, the happier we are. All questions are welcome. Of course, we can't promise all the answers, but we'll tell you what we know, we'll guide you to places that might help you find the answers, we'll tell you what we think, and we'll listen to what you think, too. It's all about sharing ideas, thoughts, information, observations, and feelings.

In many cases, in fact, questions are more important than answers. That's the thing about questions: The more you ask ... the more you ask!

Here are some other interesting aspects to the *KIDS CAN!*
NATURAL HISTORY MUSEUM:

 No one is more important than kids like you,
and all kids are equally important.

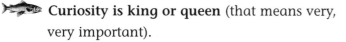 **Curiosity is king or queen** (that means very,
very important).

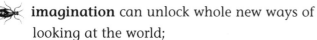 It's a place where

 imagination can unlock whole new ways of
looking at the world;

 where **your opinion** is very special;

 where **trying something new** or difficult for
you is more important than doing things that
are easy for you.

 Dig in for the fun and participate: Make
art, talk about what you see, rap a rap,
wonder aloud, join us for a dino party (see page
79), roam around, giggle and laugh, play
fossilologist and other games, build your own
Brachiosaurus skeleton, and even reconstruct a
chicken!

What Is Natural History, Anyway?

WELL, GET THIS: Natural history is everything to do with life on earth, from the start of single-celled protozoa perhaps billions of years ago to the complexities of your DNA today. It's about plants and animals, and how they grew, changed, adapted, or became extinct; about habitats, biomes, and ecosystems; about ancient cultures on all continents; it's about 50,000-year-old mummies and the kid standing right next to you now! It's about rocks, the earth, and outer space, too. Whew! *It's nature's history!*

Most people who are interested in natural history focus on specific areas that interest them, and most museums can't possibly cover everything. So relax, because we are just going to focus on the past "brief" period of animal life on earth — say the past 570 million years (that's 570,000,000!) — beginning back in the Cambrian period of the Paleozoic era and moving up to the mammals, including humans like you!

We'll save the study of plants and the glories of ancient civilizations for other museums — er — books. After all, we want you to take your time, and 570 million years of animal life seem like a lot to cover!

In the *KIDS CAN!* NATURAL HISTORY MUSEUM, you'll come face-to-face (so to speak) with

A ◆ *Archaeopteryx,* the dino-like bird

B ◆ *Brachiosaurus*

C ◆ Cambrian period with trilobites

D ◆ dinos, dinos, and more dinos

E ◆ echinoderms like starfish and sand dollars

F ◆ fossils, for sure

G ◆ geologic time, in which *Homo sapiens* (that's you!) are merely a blink of an eye.

And, natural history is also

H ◆ habitats, from oceans to deserts

I ◆ ice ages, when ice was a mile thick!

J ◆ the Jurassic period

K ◆ Kids, kiwis, kangaroos, and krill (the food of some whales)

L ◆ Linnaeus (a guy who liked to sort things)

M ◆ the Mesozoic era, when the Age of Reptiles (and they were huge!) took hold

N ◆ newts and other amphibians

O ◆ the Ordovician period, when jawless fish evolved

P ◆ pterosaurs, those amazing gliding reptiles.

And don't forget

Q ◆ the Quaternary period, when mammoths and saber-toothed tigers died out ... and you were born!

R ◆ regenerating rays (ask the starfish)

S ◆ sharks (who don't need to brush)

T ◆ *Tyrannosaurus rex,* of course!

U ◆ undersea life

V ◆ *Velociraptor*s, volcanoes, and vertebrates

W ◆ woolly mammoths (not exactly cuddly)

X ◆ xerophytes (nope, not "zero" — these plants just grow in dry habitats)

Y ◆ YOU! (You are a very important part of natural history!)

Z ◆ zoophytes (which don't live in zoos!)

Getting Oriented

GRAB HOLD OF YOUR CURIOSITY and bring along plenty of imagination. You are in an amazing museum! Are you ready? We suggest you begin at the HALL OF HOW-TO TOOLS, where a lot of your technical questions will be answered (and where your ideas may help in the search for new answers). After that, feel free to peek in any hall, or begin at the beginning and end at the end. Wherever you go, you'll find lots to do.

In the center of each hall (or on a table in your kitchen or classroom), you'll find a huge table with lots of art supplies, games, computers, and activities for you to use in your exploration of the "recent" past. You can make art, classify according to what makes most sense for you, build a "reconstruction" like the ones in natural history museums around the world, or participate however you most enjoy. Remember, everything here is for YOU! Natural history is fun and exciting — but only if *you* join in.

A *curator* has planned all of the exhibits and posted notes around to help you know where you are in time and place (it's easy to get lost in 570 million years!). There are museum guides to answer your questions in every hall. And there are even headphones that you can put on to listen to some very unusual stuff that might surprise you. To discover what some of these prehistoric animals were able to do, visit each hall's DISCOVERY CORNER, where you can actually "Try it!" Who knows? You might begin to see the animals of the world in a whole new way!

Here's a floor plan to help you find your way. Oh, yes — at 2:00 every afternoon there is a dino party just for kids in the GREAT HALL. Be sure to come for some dino cake and fun, too.

Hall of
Insects

Hall of
Sea Creatures

Hall of
Amphibians
& Reptiles

Restrooms

Hall of
How-To
Tools

Entrance

Hey, Kids!
Don't miss the
DINO PARTY
at 2:00 P.M. today
in the GREAT HALL.
Sorry, but no grown-ups
allowed!

Great Hall

Exit

DISCOVERY CORNER

Hall of
Dinosaurs

Hall of
Birds

Hall of
Mammals

← Vickie
Age 9
4½ ft.

← Tyler
Age 5
1½ ft.

Today's special
from
PHYLUM
MOLLUSCA
and
CLASS
OSTEICHTHYES

Cafeteria

WELCOME to the HALL OF HOW-TO TOOLS.

How we go about collecting information and answering questions about what happened millions — why even billions — of years ago is one of the most fascinating things about natural history. After all, how do we know what happened 570 million years ago to creatures we've never seen before?

You probably have lots of questions, such as how do we know what huge beasts looked like when all we have are some bones we've found? How do we know how old something is? How do we know if a critter had feathers or fur — or was bald?

These are all very good questions. The HALL OF HOW-TO TOOLS will give you an understanding of how we know what we know today. And it may encourage you to want to participate in what we learn in the future. So, come on in for a hands-on how-to adventure into the tools of the natural history world!

HALL OF

HOW-TO

TOOLS

A BIG "Little" Secret

Want to share a little secret? *The best way to organize information is to take big amounts of information, sort it, group it, and classify it.* Then, take each of those groups, and sort, group, and classify again. And so on and so on.

What you are doing in this simple process is seeing *relationships:* how a thing, an idea, or a time period relates to others that came before or came after, or others that share similar characteristics.

When it comes to all living animals on earth over the past 600 million years, knowing how to sort, group, classify, and see relationships is the key to being a good natural history detective. And that is what this is all about: being a great detective!

Simple sort

It doesn't matter what you are sorting: It could be photos; it could be a button collection; it could be things you collect on a trip to the beach. By sorting, grouping, and classifying — that is, finding things that make items or ideas in one group different from items or ideas in another — you get everything in manageable chunks. The more you sort, the smaller the groups. In each group, look for similar characteristics and sort out those that don't fit.

1. Take buttons, shells, leaves, rocks — whatever you have available. Look them over, and sort into two huge categories: large and small; bright colors or dark colors; buttons with four holes, those with two — whatever you think are the two biggest categories of your collection. Everything must fit in one category or the other.

Group Sort B
(small)

Group Sort A
(large)

2. Call those Group Sort A and Group Sort B. Write down the characteristics of each group.

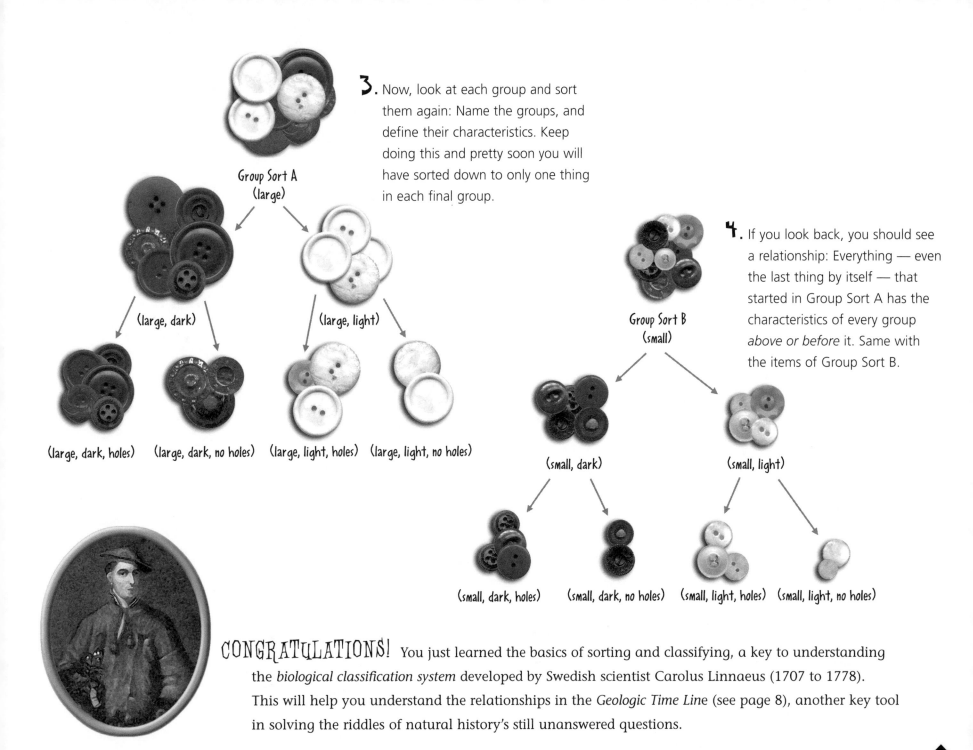

Group Sort A
(large)

3. Now, look at each group and sort them again: Name the groups, and define their characteristics. Keep doing this and pretty soon you will have sorted down to only one thing in each final group.

4. If you look back, you should see a relationship: Everything — even the last thing by itself — that started in Group Sort A has the characteristics of every group *above or before* it. Same with the items of Group Sort B.

Group Sort B
(small)

(large, dark)

(large, light)

(large, dark, holes)   (large, dark, no holes)   (large, light, holes)   (large, light, no holes)

(small, dark)

(small, light)

(small, dark, holes)   (small, dark, no holes)   (small, light, holes)   (small, light, no holes)

CONGRATULATIONS! You just learned the basics of sorting and classifying, a key to understanding the *biological classification system* developed by Swedish scientist Carolus Linnaeus (1707 to 1778). This will help you understand the relationships in the *Geologic Time Line* (see page 8), another key tool in solving the riddles of natural history's still unanswered questions.

Classification of Living Things

All living things, from tiny single-celled protozoa to gigantic whales, from algae on a pond to violets in a field to huge redwood trees, belong in the biological classification system. They are divided into five *kingdoms* — the largest groups. (This is similar to your deciding to sort leaves in one huge group, stones in another huge group, and buttons in another huge group. They would be your kingdoms.)

In our *Kids Can!* Museum, we are exploring the *animal kingdom* and some of the next subgroups called *phyla,* and then the next smaller groups called *classes.*

Here's how the classification structure looks. (Remember that everything belongs to all the groups above it, but not to the groups below it — just like in your button sort). See how *Tyrannosaurus rex* looks on this classification system:

T. rex

KINGDOM	Animalia*
PHYLUM	Chordata
CLASS	Reptilia
ORDER	Saurischia
FAMILY	Tyrannosauridae
GENUS	*Tyrannosaurus*
SPECIES	*rex*

* These are the Latin names. The English names are on page 5.

THE BIOLOGICAL CLASSIFICATION SYSTEM

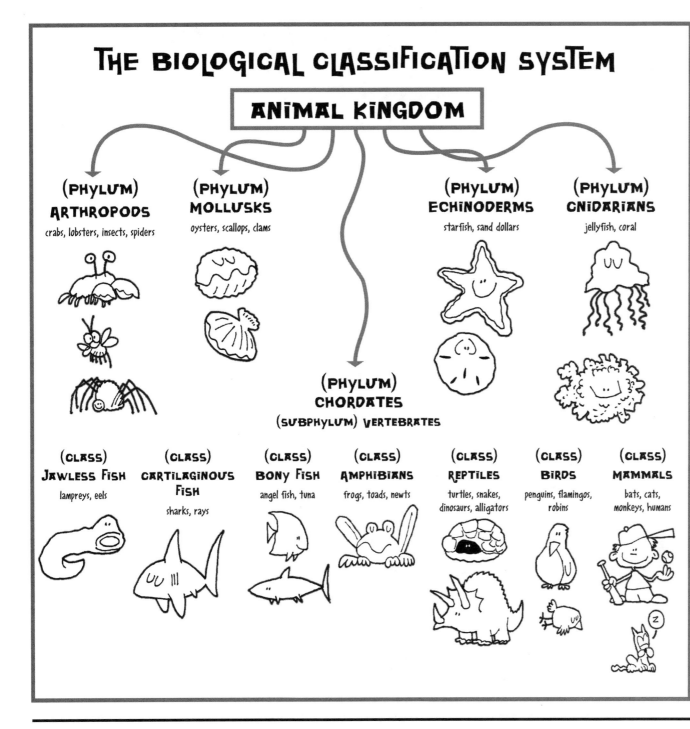

ANIMAL KINGDOM

(PHYLUM) ARTHROPODS
crabs, lobsters, insects, spiders

(PHYLUM) MOLLUSKS
oysters, scallops, clams

(PHYLUM) ECHINODERMS
starfish, sand dollars

(PHYLUM) CNIDARIANS
jellyfish, coral

(PHYLUM) CHORDATES
(SUBPHYLUM) VERTEBRATES

(CLASS) JAWLESS FISH
lampreys, eels

(CLASS) CARTILAGINOUS FISH
sharks, rays

(CLASS) BONY FISH
angel fish, tuna

(CLASS) AMPHIBIANS
frogs, toads, newts

(CLASS) REPTILES
turtles, snakes, dinosaurs, alligators

(CLASS) BIRDS
penguins, flamingos, robins

(CLASS) MAMMALS
bats, cats, monkeys, humans

Time Flies

We might just as well tackle the hard questions first, right? And nothing is more difficult for us humans to understand than time. After all, we can't see it, or touch it, or taste it, or smell it, or hear it. No wonder we have a hard time understanding it!

Have you ever heard the saying, "Time flies when you're having fun!"? Well, it's true, isn't it? Think about your favorite class in school; it sure goes by faster than your least favorite class. Yet, a clock or calendar counts them out exactly the same.

And think about how your grandparents may seem very much older than you are. In natural history, well, their 40 years more is but a fraction of a second! So let's try to get a handle on time — 570 million years of it, actually!

Before You/After You TIME LINE

You've probably seen time lines before: They divide a line into periods of time, marking when things happened in relation to one another. A lot of museums and history books use time lines because they help organize events in THE ORDER THEY HAPPENED. So let's try that, too.

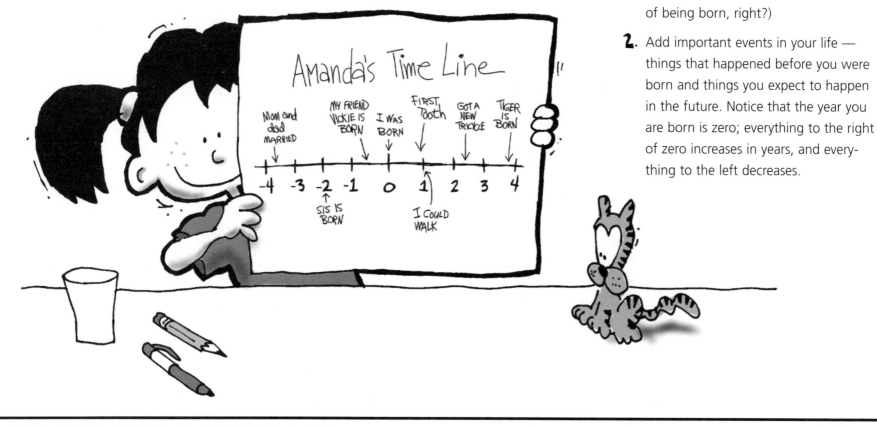

Amanda's Time Line

Mom and dad MARRIED

MY FRIEND VICKIE IS BORN

I WAS BORN

FIRST Tooth

GOT A NEW TRICYCLE

TIGER IS BORN

-4 -3 -2 -1 0 1 2 3 4

SIS IS BORN

I COULD WALK

1. Put your birth in the middle of the line, divide the line into years before you were born and after your birth, and "get your life in order!" (After all, you can't be getting your first tooth ahead of being born, right?)

2. Add important events in your life — things that happened before you were born and things you expect to happen in the future. Notice that the year you are born is zero; everything to the right of zero increases in years, and everything to the left decreases.

GEOLOGIC TIME

How do we have a time line that shows 570 million years or so? Well, that is a tricky one. The answer is called the *geologic time line* which uses both *classifying* (or grouping), as well as the *order of events.* This time line divides time into three enormous *eras (Paleozoic, Mesozoic,* and *Cenozoic),* and then breaks those down into smaller *periods.*

The geologic time line uses time + events to define each period.

Because we don't know everything about geologic time (that is for sure!), there is still a lot of disagreement about what happened when. You'll find geologic time lines don't always agree with one another. That's where the detective work comes in: people working to find more factual information that will fill in the blanks where we don't really know what happened.

As you might guess by the name geologic, a lot of evidence we find comes from the story of life on earth contained in the layers of rock and the fossil records those rocks contain studied by geologists and paleontologists.

GEOLOGIC TIME LINE

ERA	PERIOD		EVENTS	
				Now
CENOZOIC "recent life"	QUARTERNARY		Mammoths and saber-toothed tigers die out. Modern man evolves.	
	TERTIARY		"Age of Mammals"—mammals develop into many different types. Insects, birds, and flowering plants flourish. Primates evolve. First humanlike creatures.	1.6
MESOZOIC "middle life"	CRETACEOUS		First flowering plants; last of the dinosaurs, including Tyrannosaurus Rex. Mass extinction at end of the period.	65
	JURASSIC		First known bird, Archaeopteryx, appears. Dinos rule the land.	135
	TRIASSIC		Mammals and dinosaurs. Climate warms.	205
PALEOZOIC "ancient life"	PERMIAN		Reptiles spread; beetles evolve. Mass extinction (last trilobites) as earth cools.	250
	CARBONIFEROUS		Swampy forests, ferns. First winged insects and reptiles. Amphibians spread.	290
	DEVONIAN		"Age of Fish." Bony fish and sharks evolve. First amphibians appear. Trees and low green plants on land.	355
	SILURIAN		First land plants, early jawed fish.	410
	ORDOVICIAN		Jawless fish, shellfish, and invertebrates in sea.	438
	CAMBRIAN		Algae, trilobites, and early coral and starfish in sea.	510
	PRECAMBRIAN		Imprints of soft-bodied invertebrates like worms and jellyfish.	570

Geologic Time Rap . . .

We all tell time
  on a clock;
We all know rap —
  from Will Smith to Bach.
But what about that
  special time
That moves along a
  geologic line?

Time, time
  that great divide —
Its distance marked
  in years so wide.

**Geo-, geo-
  geologic time
From trilobites to me,
  (I sighed.)
It's just a hop, a skip,
  a jump,
570 myas? Why
  it's barely a bump!**

Chorus:

*Time goes from then
  all the way to now
It's hard to grasp,
  but I know how!*

First came the *Paleo-
  zoic era,*
It seemed the earth
  was barely there-uh.
"Paleo" means
  early, you know
And first they were
  so small and slow.

It started with
  those trilobites
Whose faces we see
  at fossil sites.
The era ended with
  insects galore —
I'm certain the reptiles
  weren't hoping for more!

**Paleo-, paleo-
  Paleozoic era!
It seemed the earth
  was barely there-uh!**

Chorus . . .

Then came the **Meso-zoic era**
A time in the middle
   With a reign of terror!

We know it well —
   Triassic, you say?
Oh yes, I saw
   a *Herrerasaurus* today!
And Jurassic —
   it was a walk in the park
With *Allosaurus* a-roaming
   (stay in after dark!).
Finally the period *Cre-ta-ce-ous*
When dinos disappeared,
   Oh my!
   Good gra-ci-ous!

Meso-, meso-,
   Mesozoic era!
Dinos were king, and then
   weren't there-uh!

Chorus . . .

Time goes from then
   all the way to now
It's hard to grasp,
   but I know how!

Last came the era
   known as **Cenozoic** —
A time of birth of
   the earth (as we know it).

A mere 65
   million years ago,
A time when species
   met their foe,
For many creatures then
   became extinct
We can only guess
   why their populations
   "shrinked"!
But man and woman
   like you and me —
Cenozoic is when
   we came to be!

Ceno-, ceno-
   Cenozoic time!
At last on earth
   is humankind!

Chorus . . .

FOSSILS!

What is most important to paleontologists? Well, fossils rank right up there at the top, because *fossils capture life forms from millions of years ago.* That's why we still find fossils of the Cambrian period of the Paleozoic era. Many fossils are of shelled sea creatures: The sea creature dies and its soft tissue decays, but the shell may be buried intact by sediment. Amazingly, over millions of years, the shell — or its imprint — remains in the stone that forms around it.

Some fossils, called *index fossils,* are particularly important because they provide an "index" or record in rock formations of a particular type of life in a particular time. When we find something else near a trilobite, for example, we know its date because we know when trilobites existed. Trilobites are good index fossils for the Cambrian period because they are so plentiful.

EGADS! That's a TRILOBITE?

Make a Footprint Cast

Being able to make good casts of fossils is an important field skill. (After all, you never know when you might come across an important fossil find.) Here's how to create a plaster footprint cast just like a paleontologist!

MATERIALS

Cereal-box cardboard
Tape
Large, clean can (a coffee can works well)
Plaster of paris (from a hardware store)
Container of water
Garden trowel (or other small digging tool)
Old toothbrush

LET'S DO IT!

1. Bend the cardboard into a collar shape around the footprint. Fasten the ends of the collar with tape.

2. In the can, mix 1½ parts of plaster with 1 part water. Stir. The final consistency should be like gravy or pancake batter. Do the mixing quickly (plaster hardens in no time).

3. Pour the plaster over the footprint, making sure it fills the print completely. (A little overflow is OK.) Wait 30 minutes.

4. When the plaster has hardened, carefully dig around the cast, and remove it from the ground. Clean the cast, using water and a toothbrush.

5. You now have the reverse of the actual footprint. If you want the actual print, you can make a second cast. Just coat the cast in dishwashing liquid to keep the second cast from sticking. Then, repeat steps 1 through 4 with the collar at least 1" (2.5 cm) higher than the cast.

NOTE: Please don't pour any leftover plaster down the toilet or rinse out your can in the sink. It will clog them. Wrap them in newspaper and throw them away.

Mired in Natural History . . .

Yes, much of what we know about natural history today comes from the fossils we've found. If you were an ancient woolly mammoth, here's how you might have become "stuck" in time:

TAR BEACH

Imagine wading into a pond for a cool drink on a hot day, and then getting stuck in sticky mud. Yikes! Well, that's just what appears to have happened to hundreds of woolly mammoths, bison, and other animals long ago in what is now Los Angeles, California. The animals waded in to drink rainwater on top of the tar pits and became trapped. When the tar hardened, the skeletons were preserved as fossils. A sticky situation, indeed!

FOSSILS ON ICE

A similar, but chillier fate preserved woolly mammoths in the icy tundra of northern Siberia, where they may have become mired in soft ground during a summer thaw in the tundra. Then, they became covered by ice in the next storm. Some of these "deep freeze" finds are so well preserved that scientists have figured out what the mammoth ate for its last lunch — 10,000 years ago!

Roots and Stems

A lot of words in the English language have roots and stems from Latin and Greek words. You can figure them out from the list below.

amphi (both kinds)

anthro (human)

arch (chief)

archeo (ancient)

astro (star)

bio (life, living things)

cen (new, recent)

chrono (time)

cosmos (world)

cracy (rule by)

geo (earth)

graph (write)

hydro (water)

ist (one who does something, "bicycl"ist)

logy (study of, words)

mes (middle)

meter (to measure)

micro (small)

nomy (laws of)

ophy (knowledge about)

paleo (ancient, early, dealing with fossils)

philo (love)

psyche (soul)

socio (companion)

techne (skill)

zoic (relating to a geologic era)

zoo (animals)

Using this chart you can immediately tell what a *biologist* does *(bio + logy + ist):* A biologist studies living things. What do you think a *microbiologist* does? Now can you tell what these people do: *paleontologist, anthropologist, sociologist, geologist, zoologist?* Here's a tough one for you — *paleoanthropologist?*

For fun, make up words using these roots, stems, and others that interest you. Take a single word like "auto" and see how big a tree you can "grow" using roots and stems.

PLAY Fossil-ologist!

Play what, you say? Fossil-ologist is a game based on roots and stems to play with your friends (you can practice on your own).

Using the list here — or your own list of roots and stems — create as many words as you can. Take turns saying a word with its meaning. If someone challenges you, look the word up in a dictionary. If it is a real word, you get a point; if it is a made-up word that is not in the dictionary, the challenger gets a point. If no one challenges you on a made-up word, you get two points. First player to get eight points wins.

Here's one to get you started:

"zoonomy"? Real or made-up?

NOTE: Some words may not be spelled exactly as the roots are.

How's a Dinosaur Fossil Made?

Dinosaur bone fossils, like other animal bone fossils, were made millions of years ago, after the dinosaur died and its soft parts (such as its skin and insides) rotted away, leaving only its hard parts (such as bones and teeth). Over long, long periods of time, these hard parts became buried, were covered with water, and turned to stone as the water's minerals and the sediment combined. Other dinosaur fossils were made when footprints were left in a soft place, like a muddy shore, and then filled with other sediment that hardened to form the fossilized footprint. As the rock layers of long ago eroded, the dinosaur fossils appeared and were found by people — people just like you!

TRY IT!

Bury a cleaned chicken bone (or a steak bone) and a piece of lettuce in two different places in your yard. Mark the areas with rocks so you remember where each is buried, leaving the buried objects undisturbed for two weeks. Then, uncover the objects. Which one decomposed, or rotted away, and which one remained? Which one do you think would be more likely to be found as a fossil in years to come?

Chicken BONE Tales

Some of what we know about dinosaurs and other animals comes from what their fossils tell us. But do bones tell the whole story?

MATERIALS

Bones from a whole roasted chicken or turkey

Bleach ☠ (adult use only)

LET'S DO IT!

1. Gather all of the bones after a dinner made from a whole chicken or turkey. Pick off all remaining meat.

☠ 2. Once the bones are thoroughly cleaned, ask a grown-up to soak them in some bleach. (Do not do this yourself! Bleach is poisonous.) Set them aside for about an hour. Then, ask a grown-up to remove the bones from the bleach, rinse, and allow them to dry.

3. Now, imagine you are a paleontologist who has just discovered a fossil site in your neighborhood. Unlike most fossil finds, you have all the skeletal parts on hand. Lucky you!

4. Try reassembling the chicken from the bones. (You have luck on your side again because you already know what the complete chicken looks like, unlike most paleontologists.) What do the bones tell you? Do you know how big the chicken was? How much it weighed? Anything about its skin color? What about feathers? Fur? Hair? Did it fly? Did it have two or four legs? Was it warm-blooded? Cold-blooded?

Exactly how much can bones tell?

RECONSTRUCTING *T. rex* & Friends

Most fossils — dinosaurs, for example — are not found with all the pieces in one place. Someone may find a bone here, several more a few feet away, and maybe a skull as much as a mile (or many miles) away. How do we know what the creature looked like or even if it all belongs to one creature?

It's like doing a puzzle with some of the most important pieces missing.

Or, it's like doing a puzzle where the pieces from several different puzzles have all been tossed in one box.

Quite a challenge, as you'll see ...

BRONTOSAURUS
the Dino that NEVER WAS!

A dino that had a name, but never really existed? How could that happen? Paleontologists usually work with skeletons that don't have all their parts. That's just what happened with *Brontosaurus.*

In 1879, famous fossil hunter O. C. Marsh found parts of a huge skeleton in Wyoming. The skeleton was missing a lot of pieces, including the skull, but Marsh was in a hurry to put it all together before his rival, Edward Drinker Cope, found out. Marsh drew some sketches, and then added a head that he found close by that looked like it fit the body. He named his new dino *Brontosaurus.*

About 25 years later, another paleontologist showed that *Brontosaurus* was actually the same dinosaur species as the *Apatosaurus* that Marsh, himself, had discovered two years earlier! Then, in the 1970s, paleontologist Jack McIntosh realized that the head Marsh had used was actually from a *Camarasaurus!*

This mistake has been corrected, but for about 100 years, museums and books showed the *Brontosaurus* — a dino that never existed!

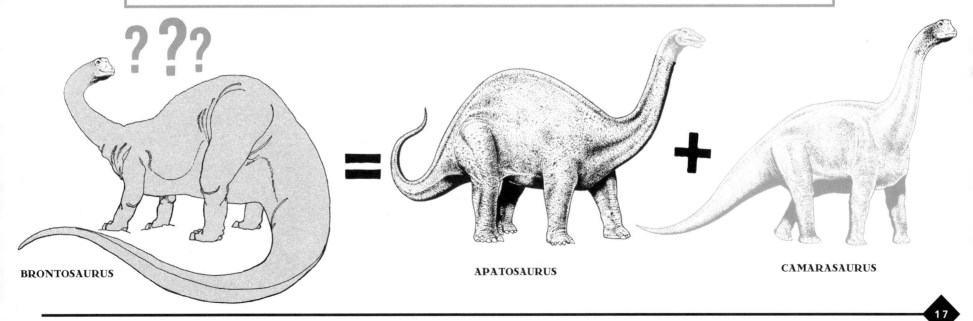

BRONTOSAURUS   **APATOSAURUS**   **CAMARASAURUS**

From Rock to Museum

There are a lot of interesting people who work around a fossil discovery. Which would you like to be?

The paleontologists:

When paleontologists uncover fossilized bones or skeletons, the position of each bone is recorded and photographs are taken at the site, or *excavation,* in order to help piece the animal back together later on. Then, each fossilized bone is encased in a layer of plaster of paris to protect it on its way to the museum.

The museum artists:

Because fossil bones are so valuable, they aren't usually used in museum exhibits. Instead, the museum artists make *replicas,* or exact copies, of them by covering the bone with a rubber-and-fiberglass mold. The real stone bones are then removed and safely stored away, and replica bones are displayed.

The reconstructionists:

The photographs of the bones are very carefully studied because the exhibit must be as accurate as possible. With dinosaur finds, for example, the dinosaur's body is constructed with steel rods, and the replica bones are attached to the rod frame with wires and screws. When the replica bones are wired together, they look just like the real fossilized skeleton!

The mounted skeleton you see when you go to a museum is called a *reconstruction* — a model of what the paleontologists think this particular real dinosaur or prehistoric animal looked like.

CLICK!

TIME-TRAVEL BACK — about 450 million years! (This natural history stuff really does take a good imagination! But if George Lucas could imagine Darth Vader in *Star Wars,* and Steven Spielberg could imagine *E.T.,* well, why not? Go for it!)

Do you suppose there would be anything living in the ocean yet?

Some scientists believe that oceans way back then had ancient coral reefs, crayfish-like critters called *trilobites,* and the ancient relatives of sea sponges, sea scorpions, jellyfish, and starfish in the water!

They aren't the same sea creatures we see today, of course, but they shared certain characteristics — number of legs, skeleton inside or out, number of main body parts — as the sea life today. By taking a closer look at the creatures around us in the here and now, we can get a better idea of what life might have been like way back then.

And as you enter the HALL OF SEA CREATURES, imagine a time when the oceans held *all* life on earth!

HALL OF

SEA
CREATURES

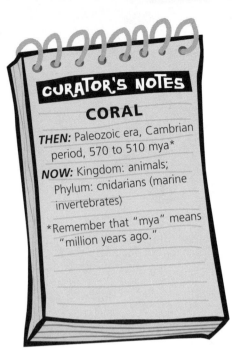

CURATOR'S NOTES

CORAL

THEN: Paleozoic era, Cambrian period, 570 to 510 mya*

NOW: Kingdom: animals; Phylum: cnidarians (marine invertebrates)

*Remember that "mya" means "million years ago."

"Brainy" Tropical Gardens

Coral colonies sometimes look like branching trees, tiny individual flowers, large domes — or miniature brains (called BRAIN CORAL, of course). Go to the activity table in the HALL OF SEA CREATURES to capture the look of two different types of coral colonies.

Coral impressions

Live coral are among the most beautiful animals in the sea, like colorful flowers in shades of tan, orange, yellow, purple, and green in an undersea tropical garden!

Using a sponge or cotton ball as your brush, capture the colorful mix of a coral garden in an undersea world. Create an *impressionist* work of art which, unlike a photo, just shows blends of colors that hint at the overall shapes. Picture the live coral swaying in the watery currents like trees in slow motion.

Brain coral replica

To make your own brain coral, shape some salt dough (mix 1½ cups/375 ml salt, 4 cups/1 liter flour, 1½ cups/375 ml water) into a fat pancake. Roll some extra dough into tiny snakes. Coil the snakes and press them into the pancake, until it is completely covered. Make indentations around the coils with a toothpick. Let air-dry overnight or bake at 300°F (150°C) until hard, but not brown. Paint pink, if you like.

What's in a Name?

Some coral looks so much like a plant that many people think live coral are plants. But you know coral are animals; like jellyfish, they are called *cnidarians,* sea creatures without a backbone that have a mouth surrounded by tentacles.

So what would you call an animal that looks like a plant? (Think of where you visit animals.) Take a guess and find the answer on the bottom of this page.

Categorizing Tip

Some of us tend to clump all animals that live in the ocean together as "fish," but actually fish are only one type of ocean-living animal (see pages 22, 31). Crabs and lobsters are in the phylum Arthropoda; clams and mussels are in the phylum Mollusca; sharks and rays are in the cartilaginous fish class; and the good old tuna and swordfish are in the "bony fish" class. And don't forget the whale — a mammal just like you!

Answer: If you said "zooplant," give yourself a pat on the back. The actual name is "zoophyte," from the Greek *phyton,* meaning "plant." (See page 14 for more on Greek and Latin words.)

ECO-ALERT !

REEFS IN DANGER

Talk about slow motion! It takes thousands of years for reefs to be built by the hard skeletons of coral animals. Sometimes the reefs grow less than an inch (cm) a year! Geologists believe the Great Barrier Reef off Queensland, Australia, has been building over ancient reef foundations millions of years old! Unfortunately, these age-old coral reefs are in danger of being destroyed by pollution, harvesting for coral jewelry, and scuba divers accidentally touching and breaking off the fragile coral.

UP CLOSE

Read *A Walk on the Great Barrier Reef* by Caroline Arnold to learn more about an amazing coral reef and the fish that live there.

< HEADPHONES TO HISTORY >

A Fishy Subject

We know for certain that marine animals lived in the Paleozoic era, that lo-o-o-n-ng stretch of geologic time from 570 to 250 mya. But exactly when certain creatures were found on earth is always open to debate (see page 7).

The "Age of Fish" refers to the Devonian period, some 410 to 355 mya, when *bony fish* (fish with a backbone and an inner skeleton) are thought to have developed. But there were marine animals in ocean waters long before that.

This is the order things are believed to have happened in the *animal kingdom* of the *Paleozoic era's* water world.

First came the *invertebrates:*
(no backbone or spinal cord)

- Soft-bodied marine life like *jellyfish* and *ancient coral*
- Fish with hard plates just below their outer skin, such as *starfish* and *sea urchins*
- *Trilobites* were common
- Soft-bodied animals with hard shells and a powerful foot, such as *scallops* and *clams*
- Animals with segmented (divided) bodies, a hard *exoskeleton* (outside the body), and multi-jointed legs, such as crabs

Today, *9 out of every 10* animals on earth are invertebrates. Imagine that!

Then came the *vertebrates:*
(animals with spinal cords or backbones)

- The most primitive fish were the *jawless fish*
- Next came *cartilaginous fish,* such as *sharks* and *rays*
- Then came the first "real" fish, the early *bony fish*

There you have it! Now, continue on for a closer look at some of the ocean creatures of today!

STARFISH stars

Have you ever seen a starfish on a beach? It probably was dead, appearing hard and stiff. Actually, a live starfish's limbs, called rays, move gracefully in the water. While most starfish have five rays, some have as many as 10 or more. No matter how many rays, the starfish always is shaped like a wheel with the rays spread out from the center (called RADIAL SYMMETRY).

And one other thing: Starfish, like all echinoderms including sand dollars, are missing something we'd all be lost without — a head!

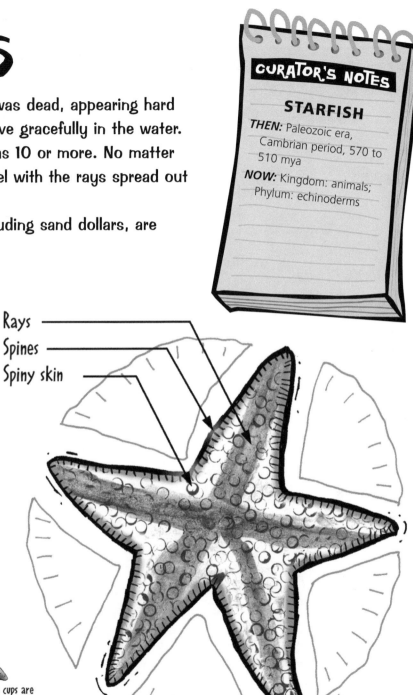

CURATOR'S NOTES

STARFISH

THEN: Paleozoic era, Cambrian period, 570 to 510 mya

NOW: Kingdom: animals; Phylum: echinoderms

Rays

Spines

Spiny skin

MATERIALS

White paper plate
Scissors
Brown tempera paint, in a dish or lid
Paintbrush
Plastic straw

LET'S DO IT!

1. Cut out a starfish from the paper plate. How many rays are you going to paint on it?

2. To make the spiny skin, dip the end of the straw into the paint; then, press small circles all around. Press more circles on the underside of the arms for *rows* of "suction cups," or tube feet.

3. Cut small fringe (spines) around the edge. Very nice!

Suction cups are
on underside

Suction Power!

If you've ever tried to open a live clam or mussel shell, you know it's very difficult. But for a starfish, it is all in a day's dinner! The rays are lined on the underside with rows of suction tubes that help the starfish pull open the shells of its prey (oysters and clams). Talk about suction power!

TRY IT!

To get an idea of starfish suction, dip the end of a plastic straw in water; then, press the wet end against a dime. Suck in hard, until you lift up the dime. That's suction at work! Here's what happened: As you inhaled, the water sealed the joint. The air pressure inside the straw was reduced, pulling the dime up against the straw. You've got starfish power!

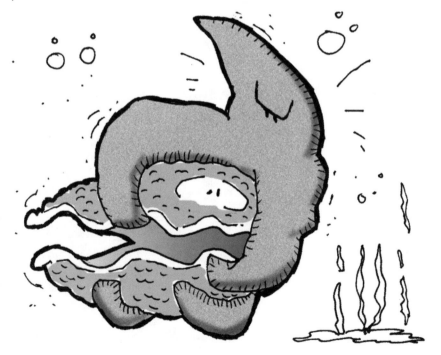

You Can't Fool Mother Nature!

Oyster fishermen used to cut up starfish to kill them because the starfish not only ate oysters, but also they got caught in the fishermen's nets. Can you guess what happened?

When a starfish loses a ray, it simply grows a new one in its place! This tricky feat is called *regeneration.* If we lose a limb, we can't grow a new one, of course, but our body's cells do regenerate new cells to replace old cells. (Think about the last time you scraped yourself.) So, how wise were those clever fishermen? Not very; the starfish population more than doubled!

CURATOR'S NOTES

GIANT SCALLOP

THEN: Paleozoic era, Ordovician period, 510 to 438 mya

NOW: Kingdom: animals; Phylum: mollusks

Giant SCALLOP

A mollusk (not a fish) that lives in ocean water, the giant scallop has a soft body, enclosed in two shell halves. And, say hello to oysters, mussels, clams, squids, and octopuses — the scallop's relatives also in the mollusk family! Yes, octopuses are advanced mollusks — it's just that they are inside out with their shells surrounded by their bodies!

MATERIALS

Scissors

Small white paper plates, 2

Crayons or markers

Transparent tape

Cotton balls

White craft glue

LET'S DO IT!

1. Cut out two scallop shells from the paper plates, using the ridged rim of each plate as the shells' edges. Color the outside of the shells.

2. Lay the scallop shells "open," flat end to flat end. Tape ends, so the shells stay together but can still open and close.

3. Open the shells wide; glue some cotton balls inside.

SITE WORKS

Start a Collection!

Nature has a lot of things that should be left where they are — like anything alive — but, as far as we know, mollusk shells are one thing you can collect to your heart's content. So go to it! It's a great way to collect things on site; sort, group, and classify them; and look up their genus and species names in a shell book. Then, clean and dry the shells. Display them on a shelf or on a pretty dish.

NOTE: Please don't take shells if an animal is living inside. The animals inside will die, and the shells will smell like rotten fish!

Crabby CRABS

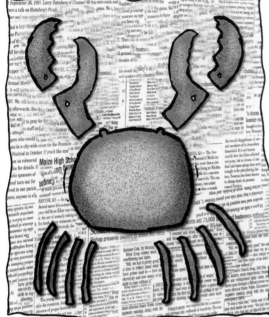

Did anyone ever call you a "crab" or accuse you of being "crabby"? Real crabs have 10 legs (five pairs), with the first pair larger than the rest, just like its crustacean relative, the lobster. These larger legs have two, big, thick pincer claws on the end that help with movement, feeding, and protection. Have any ideas about that "crabby" mood yet?

MATERIALS

Newspaper
Scissors
White paper plates, 2 large
Orange and black tempera paint, in dishes or lids

Paintbrush
Old toothbrush
Paper fasteners, 2
White craft glue
Good idea: Wear an art shirt.

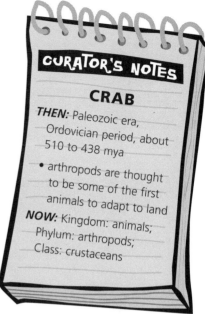

CURATOR'S NOTES

CRAB

THEN: Paleozoic era, Ordovician period, about 510 to 438 mya

• arthropods are thought to be some of the first animals to adapt to land

NOW: Kingdom: animals; Phylum: arthropods; Class: crustaceans

LET'S DO IT!

1. Cover the table with newspaper. Cut out the crab's body, legs, claws, and pincers from the large paper plates and paint them orange. Allow to dry.

2. Dip the toothbrush into the black paint. Holding the brush over the crab, run a finger across the bristles (away from you) to spatter the paint.

3. Use the paper fasteners to attach the pincers to the claws. Then, glue the claws and legs to the underside of the crab.

4. Now, try to get your crab to pick up a pencil in its pincers!

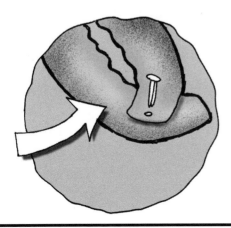

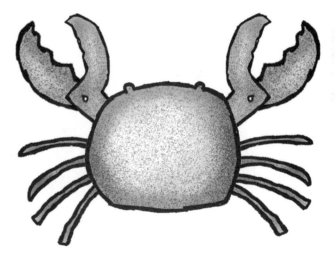

O, Give Me a Home

Hermit crabs aren't really hermits at all. In fact, they are very friendly — so friendly that they make themselves quite at home inside empty shells from snails and other shelled sea creatures. When a hermit crab outgrows its shell, it moves into a bigger shell that's been abandoned. Waste not, want not!

TRY IT!

Walk along the wet sand or some tide pools at the ocean to see hermit crabs carrying their temporary "houses" on their backs, as they skitter sideways across the sand. Sometimes you can even follow their "tracks" in the sand. Or, visit a pet store or aquarium to see hermit crabs in action!

ARTHROPOD FAMILY REUNION

Ah . . . Arthropods!

Crabs belong to the phylum arthropod.

Who else is an arthropod besides the crab? Well, if your crab looks like a spider to you, you're right! Spiders (arachnids), insects, and centipedes are all arthropods, too (see the HALL OF INSECTS AND ARACHNIDS). Does that sound like a lot of critters to you? Almost 80 percent of all animal species fall into the arthropod phylum!

So what can we conclude about arthropods? That they *don't* all live in water like those arthropods that are crustacean cousins, crabs and lobsters!

Be a Crab!

Be a crab! Be a crab! (Notice we didn't say, "Be crabby!") Here's a fun game to play at the beach — or just about anywhere!

Divide into teams. The first one in each line — the crab — sits on the floor, back facing the finish line. At the "go" signal, the crab walks backward on hands and feet, lifting hips off the ground. When the crab reaches the finish line, he or she stands up, runs back, and tags the next crab, who then takes a turn. The first team of crabs to finish wins. But don't be crabby if you lose — it's all for fun!

ECO-ALERT !

HOME, SWEET HOME

It's tempting to take live hermit crabs and other creatures such as starfish home in a bucket after visiting the beach. But even if you carefully fill your bucket with sand, water, and seaweed, your sea creatures won't survive. Most times, they'll die before you even get home! Sea creatures need their ocean home, with its just-right temperature and oxygen-rich water, to survive. You can enjoy playing with them at the water's edge or in small tide pools, but leave them in their homes when it's time for you to go to yours. Thanks, from all your seaside friends!

SPLAT!

FINISH

SHARK JAWS!

Did you ever hear of the movie JAWS? Guess what that pretend story was about? The powerful jawbone of a shark is lined with rows of sharp teeth. As one row of teeth is lost, new, sharper teeth appear from the back row — new teeth about every 10 days! (Guess sharks don't need to worry about brushing!) A shark uses up thousands of teeth every year. When a shark attacks large prey, it clamps its teeth on its victim and shakes its head from side to side.

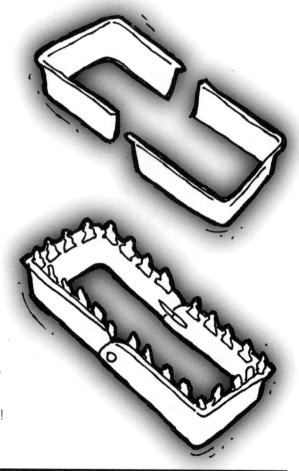

MATERIALS

Scissors
Styrofoam egg-carton lid
Paper fasteners, 2
White paper plate
White craft glue

LET'S DO IT!

1. Cut the egg-carton lid in half; then, cut away the hump, removing the center of each half and leaving the sides in place. Re-attach the lid halves with a paper fastener on each side. (The lid should move up and down.)

2. Cut out serrated teeth from the paper plate. Glue teeth around the inside edge of the lids. If you wish, make a second row, behind the first. Now, chomp away!

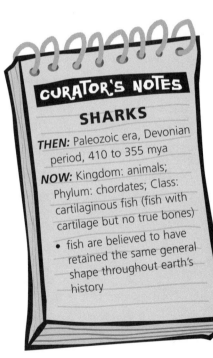

CURATOR'S NOTES

SHARKS

THEN: Paleozoic era, Devonian period, 410 to 355 mya

NOW: Kingdom: animals; Phylum: chordates; Class: cartilaginous fish (fish with cartilage but no true bones)

- fish are believed to have retained the same general shape throughout earth's history

Staying Afloat

Ever wonder how fish stay afloat? *Bony fish* (like salmon and tuna) have a *swim bladder* (sort of like a built-in life preserver) that keeps them afloat. But sharks are very different from most other fish. As *cartilaginous fish*, their skeletons are made of hard *cartilage* (like you have in your nose) instead of bones. And, they don't have a swim bladder.

So how does a shark keep from sinking? Oil in its liver helps it stay afloat. Since oil is lighter than water, the oil helps keep the shark from sinking. Even so, most sharks must swim constantly, because if they stop, their weight would pull them down to the bottom.

TRY IT!

Fill a glass halfway with water; then, drip vegetable oil on top. Where does the oil go? Now you know why you always have to shake oil and vinegar salad dressing before you pour it on a salad!

Go FISH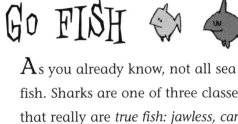

As you already know, not all sea critters are fish. Sharks are one of three classes (groups) that really are *true fish: jawless, cartilaginous,* and *bony.* All three classes share certain characteristics that make them fish.

1. They are *vertebrate* animals (they have either cartilage or a backbone).

2. They get oxygen from the water through *gills* (which allows them to stay under the water).

3. They use *fins for swimming* and most have scales (though our friends the sharks have toothlike structures buried in their skin instead).

4. They are *cold-blooded:* The temperature of their body changes with the temperature of the water. So in warm water, they have a higher temperature; in cold water, it is lower.

And, of course, all fish do not live in salt water. Many live in freshwater in lakes, rivers, and ponds. In fact, bony fish may have first developed in freshwater rivers and then later moved into salt water.

To find out more about the differences between fish and other sea life, see the whales on pages 105–107 and the sea turtles on pages 56–58.

The Better to Eat You With, My Dear!

You might think that the ancient ancestors of today's sharks looked pretty funny. *Stethacanthus* had a periscope-like knob — right in the middle of its back! *Hybodus* was 6' (2 m) long and had two sharp front teeth. And yes, sharks had powerful jaws, even way back then!

TRY IT!

Some sharks today have very descriptive names, such as cat shark, hammerhead shark, blue shark, and thresher (think "thrashing") shark. Draw pictures of what you think these sharks look like, based on their unusual names. You can draw a scientific drawing meant to look exactly like the shark, or you can draw a caricature that exaggerates certain features — like a head really shaped like a hammer going thunk!

Caricature

Scientific drawing

Hmm … Are humans warm-blooded or cold-blooded? What's your temperature in a warm bathtub and out in the snow?

(answer below)

★ **Land Ho!** As life evolved in the sea, the first plants grew on land, providing food for creatures of the land and air. Continue on to another hall — perhaps the HALL OF INSECTS AND ARACHNIDS (spiders) — to see how the great diversity of life on earth grew in new directions!

Answer: It's about 98.6°F (37°C) inside and outside. So we mammals are warm-blooded, because our temperature doesn't change with our environment's temperature (the way a fish's does).

WHAT DO YOU PICTURE when you think of an animal? Your favorite dog or cat? Or maybe even a fish? Believe it or not, the most common animal on earth doesn't fall into *any* of those groups. Think buzz, buzz instead. That's right — our planet is teeming with so many insects that they're the most common animal life! (Sorry, Fido and Boots — you're outnumbered.)

You can find insects everywhere, from deserts to jungles, in soil, swamps, caves ... even in your closet! And while you may not appreciate *all* their habits, you'd miss insects and their friends the *arachnids* (better known to you as spiders), if they weren't around. It's true! But go see for yourself — and make up your own mind about whether they are friend or foe!

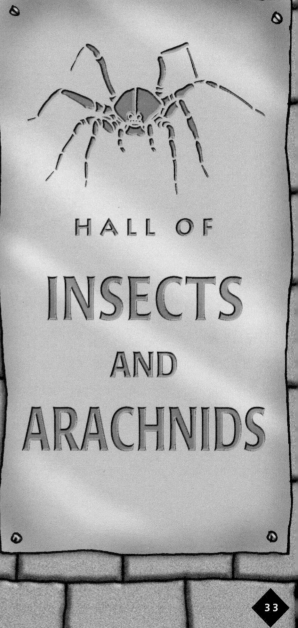

HALL OF

INSECTS
AND
ARACHNIDS

Insect Draw

You can play this game inside or out, with two or more players. All you need are a piece of paper and pencil for each player, and one die for the group.

THE GAME:

Each number on the die represents a different part of the insect's body:

- ⚀ for the head
- ⚁ for the thorax
- ⚂ for the abdomen
- ⚃ for each antenna
- ⚄ for each wing
- ⚅ for each leg

THE OBJECT:

To be the first one to draw a complete insect.

THE PLAY:

Players take turns rolling the die to draw their insect. The tricky part is that you can't add to the insect until you have the three main body parts (head, thorax, and abdomen) in place. Once you have those, you can add antennae, legs, and wings, *one at a time*, until you complete your insect (so you'll need to roll a six — six times for six legs — and so on).

What's Special About Insects?

They all have six legs (three pairs), a pair of *antennae*, and their bodies are divided into *three parts*: a *head*, *thorax* (middle), and *abdomen* (stomach). Most insects have some sort of wings — in fact, they were the first creatures to fly!

How can you tell insects from other arthropods? *Go to what you know!* Is a spider an insect? Hmmm ... did you ever see a spider with antennae? How many legs — six or eight? How about a lobster? Well, it has an exoskeleton and jointed legs, so it must be an arthropod, but it has 10 legs and no wings. Nope, it's not an insect! See, once you know a few *characteristics* of any grouping, you can begin to sort, group, and classify on your own!

head

antennae

eye

middle leg

thorax

hind leg

front leg

wing

abdomen

cercus

expensive sneakers

Make a DRAGONFLY

Delicate dragonflies only munch on other insects, not people. Their two pairs of lacy wings are downright ingenious! Each pair moves separately, like a helicopter's blades, enabling the dragonfly to hover, fly backward, and change directions at high speeds. Mother Nature sure is clever!

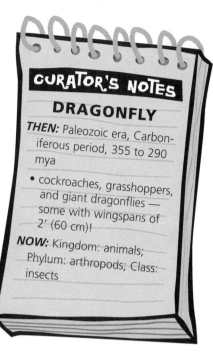

DRAGON-FLY?

MATERIALS

Cereal-box cardboard

Scissors

Green marker

Black construction paper scraps

White craft glue

Clear plastic deli lid

Black permanent marker

LET'S DO IT!

1. Cut out a three-part dragonfly body from the cardboard. Color the body green, and draw bulging eyes on the end of the head.

2. Cut out six legs from construction paper. Glue underneath the dragonfly's body.

3. Cut out the dragonfly's wings from the deli lid. Use the permanent marker to draw on thin, lacy veins. Then, glue the wings to the top of the body. Now, help your dragonfly hover and fly!

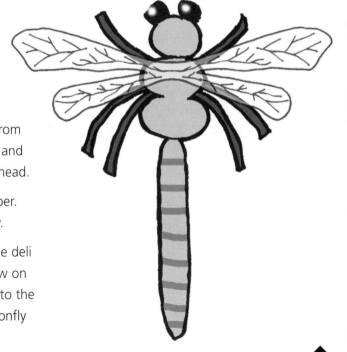

Stuck in Time

Ancient dragonflies have been found encased in amber — the fossilized sap of ancient pine trees that grew on earth more than 40 million years ago! Insects attracted to amber's sweet scent became stuck in the sticky sap. When the sap hardened to resin, the insects were trapped forever, like jewels.

TRY IT!

Ask a grown-up to help you make your own insect-in-amber. Follow the directions on a box of lemon or orange gelatin. Pour it into an ice-cube tray. Just before the gelatin sets, press gummy candy "insects" down into it. When the gelatin is firm, you'll have "insects" in "amber"— and a tasty dessert, too!

Don't BUG ME!

We call a lot of insects "bugs." But *true bugs* are a kind of insect that have a special beaklike tool for feeding and a special type of front wing.

A lady*bug* is not really a bug — it's a *beetle*. (A better name for it is "lady-bird beetle.") And believe it or not, lightning bugs (fire-flies) aren't really bugs *or* flies; they're beetles, too!

In fact, if it seems that there are a lot of kinds of beetles — well, there *are* a lot! Beetles are the largest *order* of insects on earth! There are over *one billion* beetles on earth for every human, if you can imagine that!

Lovely LADYBUG

What's the one insect that most people like to have crawling on them? Why, it's the ladybug! Ladybugs don't bite people, but they love to eat garden pests, especially aphids. Farmers actually buy them so they can put them in their fields and orchards to protect their crops — naturally!

MATERIALS

Small white paper plates, 2
Scissors
Red tempera paint, in dish or lid
Paintbrush
White craft glue
Black construction paper
Black marker

LET'S DO IT!

1. Cut away the ridged rim from two paper plates; then, cut out the ladybug's wings from one plate and the body from the other.

2. Paint the ladybug's wings and body red. Allow to dry; then, glue wings to the top of the ladybug's body.

3. Cut out six legs, two antennae, and several spots from black construction paper.

4. Glue the spots onto the wings, antennae onto the head, and legs onto the underside of body. Use the marker to draw the ladybug's eyes.

CURATOR'S NOTES

LADYBUG

THEN: Paleozoic era, Permian period, 290 to 250 mya

NOW: Kingdom: animals; Phylum: arthropods; Class: insects; Order: Coleoptera (beetles)

RED

Home, Sweet Comb

OK, honeybees do have a nasty sting and we're certainly not suggesting that you try to get up close and personal with one. In fact, a good place to see a real honeycomb without getting stung (we can learn a lot from Winnie-the-Pooh!) is in your grocery store. There you can find honey with the waxy-looking honeycomb right in a jar.

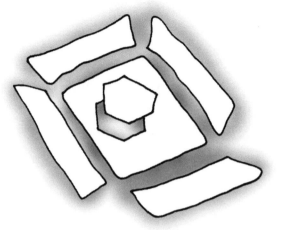

MATERIALS

Scissors	Paintbrush
Styrofoam tray (from fruits or vegetables)	Orange tempera paint, in a dish or lid
White craft glue	Clear plastic deli lid
Yellow construction paper	Permanent black marker
Cereal-box cardboard	Black and yellow pipe cleaners

LET'S DO IT!

1. Cut away the sides of the tray; then, cut out a six-sided shape (a hexagon) from the center.

2. Glue construction paper onto the cardboard.

3. Paint the hexagon; then, press onto paper for an orange beehive pattern. Cut around the edge.

4. Cut out the bee's wings from the deli lid. Use permanent marker to draw on thin veins.

5. Cut the pipe cleaners in half. Hold the black and yellow halves together while tightly wrapping them around a pencil; then, slide them off in one coil. Glue the wings onto the coil; glue the bee onto the hive.

Do You Wanna Dance?

Bees dance? It's true! When a bee finds food, it returns to its hive and performs a special dance. If the food is close to the hive, the bee does a "round" dance, and if it's far away, it dances a figure-eight, or "waggle dance." The other bees, by observing the type and speed of the dance and the angle (position) of the dancer's body, know where to head to find the food. Bees sure do some fancy footwork to get their dinner!

TRY IT!

Imagine it is a beautiful summer day with flowers in full bloom. Using pastel chalks, color a background of summer colors. Then, dip a toothpick in some tempera paint and show the flight of the bee and its dance, telling its colony where the food is to be found.

Food close to hive

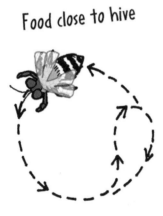

ROUND DANCE

Food farther away

WAGGLE DANCE

Make Your Own Water Lily

Plant and animal life developed in relation with one another. Bees needed the pollen of plants, and as animals moved out of water (early amphibians), plants were found at the water's edge.

Early flowering plants lived close to the shoreline of ponds and streams, and in swampy areas. The water lily, one of the earliest flowering plants, actually sinks its roots into the muddy bottom; its long stem shoots up to hold the leaves and flower on top of the water.

Here's a lily you can fold out of paper or a napkin — and it will float over a dinner plate or on your desk!

MATERIALS

One square paper or cloth napkin per lily

Optional: green construction paper, scissors, and paper fasteners

LET'S DO IT!

1. It is important that the napkin be square when unfolded. Small paper napkins are easiest to use.

2. Make three sets of folds: First, fold each of the four corners of the opened napkin into the center making a small square.

3. Next, fold in the corners again, making a smaller square.

4. Then, turn the napkin over. Fold the corners into the center one more time.

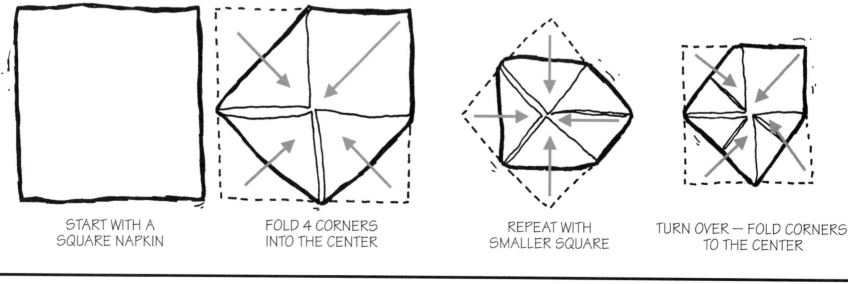

START WITH A SQUARE NAPKIN

FOLD 4 CORNERS INTO THE CENTER

REPEAT WITH SMALLER SQUARE

TURN OVER — FOLD CORNERS TO THE CENTER

PULL UP POINTED FLAP
UNDERNEATH TO FROM PETAL

Hello. Could I interest you in some pollen?

ACME POLLEN

A Perfect Trade

Bees and butterflies perform a very important job as they hunt for lunch. As pollinators, they collect nectar and pollen (the flower "dust" that makes people sneeze in the spring) for their hives, carrying pollen from flower to flower as they do so. And it's that exchange of pollen that helps the flowers develop seeds and fruit!

Without the help of bees and other insect pollinators, flowering plants wouldn't be able to survive … and without flowering plants, bees would have nothing to eat. It's a perfect partnership!

5. To make the petals, hold your folded napkin in place with one hand in the center. With your other hand, bend one of the corners toward the center. You will see a pointed flap underneath. Lift the flap with your fingers, while you push your thumb on the bent-up corner. When you've done all four corners, your lily will have four petals.

6. Turn over your almost-finished lily. Pull out the four pointed corners in the center, making four more petals.

7. To add green lily pads, cut out a scalloped circle a little bigger than the lily from green construction paper. Place the lily on the lily pad, and stick a paper fastener through the middle of both, or glue in place.

PULL OUT
4 POINTED CORNERS

LILY PAD

Magical Monarch
METAMORPHOSIS

We all like to look back at pictures of ourselves when we were younger and see how much we've grown and changed. But if you were a butterfly, you wouldn't even recognize yourself! A butterfly goes through four completely different life stages — *egg, larva (caterpillar), pupa,* and *adult* — in a magical process called

metamorphosis!

1. In the late spring and summer, look for monarch butterfly caterpillars (they're easy to spot with their black, yellow, and white stripes) on milkweed plants in fields, pastures, and meadows. Big holes in the milkweed leaves (the *only* food that the caterpillars eat) may mean the caterpillars are hiding there.

2. When you find a caterpillar, break off the leaf on which it sits, and place it in a medium-sized cardboard box, along with a branch and plenty of fresh milkweed leaves. Then, cover the box with a piece of screening or some cheesecloth. Clean your box every day, and replace old milkweed leaves with new leaves.

3. Observe your caterpillar each day with a magnifying glass. After several days it will stop eating and attach itself to the twig or top of the container. Watch for 8 to 14 days as the *chrysalis* (pupa) changes color from green to black to orange. Then, watch for the adult monarch butterfly to emerge!

4. Once it does, set the container out in the garden, where the butterfly's wings will dry, and watch it fly away!

... and They're Off!

Every year, at the end of the summer in North America, millions of monarch butterflies in Canada and the United States fly southward, migrating to winter resting grounds as far as 2,000 miles (3,218 km) away in central Mexico and California! Then, in the spring, the monarchs journey north again. It's an amazing flight, especially for a creature that weighs less than a dime!

How do you suppose those delicate insects know their way to a place none of them have ever been before? Some scientists believe monarchs have a built-in alarm clock and compass that help guide them to their winter nesting sites. No road maps? No problem!

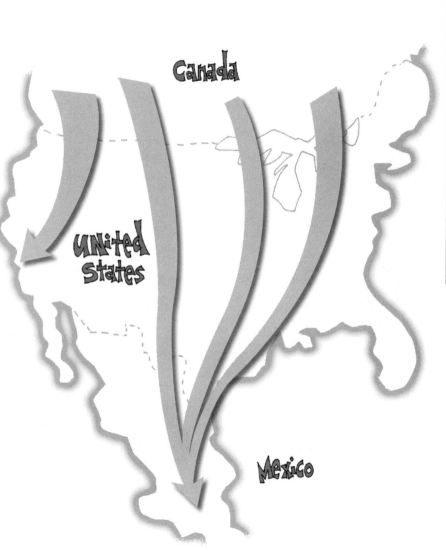

Are we there yet?

Canada

United States

Mexico

ECO-ALERT !

HOME?

Unfortunately, much of the monarch butterfly's natural habitat — the place where it grows from egg to adult, and where it lives in winter — is being destroyed. For ideas about how you can help the monarch, or to find out more about their wondrous life cycle, read *Monarch Magic!* by Lynn Rosenblatt.

< HEADPHONES TO HISTORY >

Aren't Spiders Just a Kind of Insect?

Well, no, but — sort of! How's that for a confusing answer? Think of what you know about natural history, and geologic time and the classification system. You see, that's where the "no, but sort of" answer comes in.

Insects and spiders both belong to the same phylum, Arthropod. And while we're at it, so do centipedes, grasshoppers, ants, and those spidery looking crustaceans we met in the HALL OF SEA CREATURES. Yes, they are all arthropods. They all share the characteristics of *multi-jointed, segmented limbs, segmented bodies,* and an *exoskeleton.* And they have *paired appendages* (legs), but not always the same number.

SPIDERS	VS.	INSECTS
4 pairs	LEGS	3 pairs
none	ANTENNAE	1 pair
none	WINGS	yes
exo	SKELETON	exo

It is believed that arthropods were the first animals to adapt to land millions of years ago. The very earliest insects were believed to appear after the centipedes in the *Silurian period* (438 to 410 mya). Then, in the *Devonian period,* it was "Hello, Charlotte!" as arachnids (spiders) appeared. Finally, the airborne insects, including dragonflies and grasshoppers, appeared in huge numbers in the *Carboniferous period,* 355 to 290 mya. (See page 35).

So that's why spiders and insects are not the same, but they are related. Got it? Great!

Climbing Spiders

Get an up-close view of a spider with this crawling critter.

MATERIALS

Cereal-box cardboard
Scissors
Tape

Crayons or markers
Pipe cleaners, 4
Drinking straw

1 yard (1 m) of string

LET'S DO IT!

1. Draw two circles on the cardboard, one (the abdomen) 4" (10 cm) across and the other (the head) 2" (5 cm) across. Cut out and tape together on both sides. Color a design on the spider's front.

2. Tape four pipe cleaners to the back of the head, just above where it joins the abdomen.

Bend the legs in the middle so two pairs point forward and two point backward.

3. Cut two 1" (2.5 cm) pieces from the straw. Carefully tape them (without squashing them) to the middle of the spider's back, pointing toward the head, about 1" (2.5 cm) apart.

4. Thread the string through each of the straw pieces, starting near the head. Leave a little of each end hanging below the body.

5. Hang your spider by the looped string threaded through the drinking straws over a doorknob. Gently pull the ends of the strings away from each other and watch your little climber go!

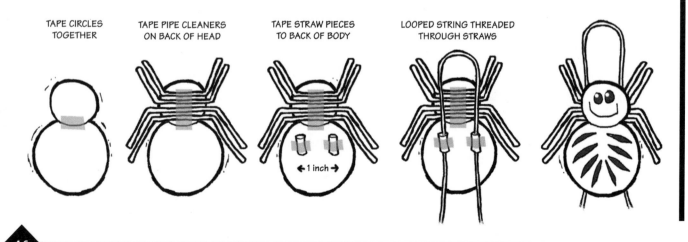

TAPE CIRCLES TOGETHER

TAPE PIPE CLEANERS ON BACK OF HEAD

TAPE STRAW PIECES TO BACK OF BODY

← 1 inch →

LOOPED STRING THREADED THROUGH STRAWS

Moving On!

Where to next? May we suggest that we leave the invertebrates and move along to greet frogs, toads, 'gators, and more *vertebrates* (animals with backbones) in the HALL OF AMPHIBIANS AND REPTILES? See you there.

DO YOU LIKE TO LOOK for tadpoles and salamanders? Or to follow a garden snake as it slithers through the grass? Whether you like to meet these critters in their natural habitats or from a respectful distance at a zoo, you're in for a treat as you enter the HALL OF AMPHIBIANS AND REPTILES at the *KIDS CAN!* NATURAL HISTORY MUSEUM.

Here, you'll explore the world of hopping toads and frogs, turtles, alligators — even rattlesnakes! These animals aren't fish; they're certainly not insects; and you can probably tell quite clearly that they aren't much like your dog or cat, either. As *amphibians* and *reptiles*, they're something else: descendants of some of the first animals to hop, run, and slither on land!

HALL OF

AMPHIBIANS

AND

REPTILES

FROG JUMP

Watching real frogs and toads hop, you quickly see the difference in how their legs stretch out. But no doubt about it, they are both great hoppers! You can have a hoppin' good time with this miniature leaping frog!

MATERIALS

8½" x 11" (21 x 25 cm) sheet of paper
Scissors
Green and black markers or crayons
Wiggly eyes (optional)

LET'S DO IT!

1. Cut the paper into an 8½" x 8½" (21 x 21 cm) square. Then, fold it in half — first one way and then the other — so the paper is equally divided into four squares. Next, fold each corner into the center.

2. With a point of the new square shape at the top, fold the outside edges into the center line, so they meet in the middle.

3. Fold up the bottom triangle, and then fold in the bottom corners to meet in the center of the bottom edge.

4. Next, fold the bottom edge up, and fold it back down on itself. Finally, fold down the point of the top triangle.

5. Color the frog green, and draw or glue on eyes. Then, hop away!

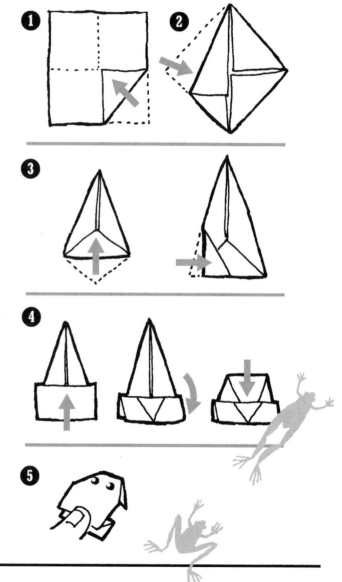

Hatch Amphibian Eggs

If you've ever watched a tadpole develop into a frog, you know just how amazing its life cycle is: first a jelly-like mass of eggs, then tiny, fishlike tadpoles, and finally, leaping frogs!

Amphibians make their way to ponds and other watery places to mate in the spring, so that's the best time to find their eggs.

TRY IT!

Take a pail to a pond or other wet area (with a grown-up, of course). You'll find frogs' eggs bunched together in a mass; toads' eggs are arranged in long strands. Bring a few eggs home in your pail, along with some pond or marsh water, and plants or algae for the tadpoles to eat.

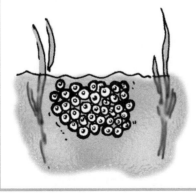

The eggs will grow and change into tadpoles in a week or two. Watch as the hind legs and tiny front legs develop. Inside the tadpole, lungs are developing to replace its fishlike *gills*. Incredible! It's moving from a water world to a land world!

Once the legs begin to grow, transfer your young amphibians to a terrarium or a cardboard box lined with plastic bags. Include a shallow container of water, some twigs, and moss. Cover with a screen, and keep it out of the sun. As cold-blooded animals (page 31), amphibians can't regulate their body temperature, so it's up to you to make sure they don't get too hot.

As soon as your frog or toad begins to crawl or hop around, enjoy it for an afternoon and then *return it to its natural home. Please don't keep one as a pet.* Thanks for doing your part to keep the frogs and toads safe and sound!

Frog and Toad Are Friends . . . But Different!

If you've read *Frog and Toad Are Friends* by Arnold Lobel, you know how different these two storybook amphibian friends really are. (Human friends — even best friends — have lots of differences, too.)

To tell frogs and toads apart, look closely.

FROG	TOAD
Smooth, shiny, slimy skin ◆	◆ Rougher, warty-looking skin
Long legs, good for long leaps ◆	◆ Shorter legs, for shorter hops
Lives in or near water or wet areas ◆	◆ Lives in shaded gardens and woodsy areas
Lays eggs in masses ◆	◆ Lays eggs in strands
Sharp, little teeth ◆	◆ No teeth
Brown tadpoles ◆	◆ Black tadpoles

Double Agents!

The name *amphibian* means "double life" (it comes from the Greek words *amphi* + *bio,* see page 14). Amphibians spend periods of their lives on land and other periods in or near water.

Bet you can figure out how *amphibious vehicles* got their name!

Pin the "Scale" on the Reptile?

Here's a twist on a favorite game that takes skill and quick thinking!

THE SETUP:

Draw a frog on green construction paper and a snake on brown construction paper. Pin them on a wall, or tape them to the refrigerator at chest height.

On *individual* strips of white paper, write down the following clues:

AMPHIBIAN CLUES

- Moist, porous skin
- Soft, jelly-like eggs
- Spend part of life in water
- Young (tadpoles) breathe through gills
- Vertebrate

REPTILE CLUES

- Dry, scaly, water-proof skin
- Eggs with shells
- Young have lungs
- Babies are parent miniatures!
- Vertebrate

TO PLAY:

Only two play at a time. Each player takes a clue — one at a time. The player then tries to pin the clue on the correct picture. Take turns until all the clues are used up. The player with the most clues on the correct animal — amphibian or reptile — wins.

CURATOR'S NOTES

REPTILES

THEN: Paleozoic era, Carboniferous period, 355 to 290 mya

- first reptiles — small lizard-like creatures

NOW: Kingdom: animals; Phylum: chordates; Class: reptiles

- includes lizards, turtles, snakes, crocodiles

< HEADPHONES TO HISTORY >

Ancient Reptiles

As reptiles evolved over millions and millions of years, some became bigger ... and bigger ... and really big, while others became legless or adapted to life in the water.

During the Mesozoic era (250 mya), dinosaurs were king — but they weren't the only show around. Over millions of years, reptiles adapted to all sorts of different lifestyles. Winged reptiles called *pterosaurs* glided in the sky along with enormous dragonflies and other flying insects. Gigantic sea reptiles called *plesiosaurs* and *pliosaurs* swam in the ocean along with sharks, lungfish, and other sea life. And *ichthyosaurs,* fishlike reptiles with dolphinlike snouts and tails frolicked in the seas, too. They were all part of the wonderful diversity and adaptation, or *evolution,* happening very slowly over millions of years to life on earth!

ENORMOUS DRAGONFLY

PTERODACTYLUS

PLESIOSAURUS

COELACANTH (ANCIENT FISH)

ICHTHYOSAURUS

Gliding PTERANODONS!

It's a bird, it's a plane, it's a ... reptile? The PTERANODON was a PTEROSAUR, a gliding reptile that lived during dinosaur times. It had a turkey-sized body with a long, long head that was the size of a man — 6' (2 m) long from the tip of its long, toothless beak to the end of a long, bony, crest! And its wings reached as wide as a house! Can you picture all that attached to such a small body?

CURATOR'S NOTES

PTERANODONS

THEN: Mesozoic era, 250 to 65 mya

• gliding reptiles; distant cousins to dinosaurs

MATERIALS

Scissors
Large white paper plates
Black marker
Paper tube
White craft glue
Transparent tape
Paint

LET'S DO IT!

1. Cut out the head, legs, and wings from paper plates. Then, draw a face.

2. Glue the wings across the top of the tube. Cut a ½" (1 cm) slit through one end of the tube and slide in the head and neck. Tape to hold.

3. Glue or tape legs inside the tube at the opposite end of the head. Color with the black marker, and then help your *Pteranodon* glide!

Slit

Artful ALLIGATOR

Both 'gators and crocs have a thick-skinned body covered in hard scales. With their webbed feet, they're both at home in the water. Just in case you wondered which is which, alligators have wide, flat heads and a blunt, wide snout; crocodiles usually have long, triangle-shaped heads.

Still stumped? An alligator's upper teeth are easy to see when its jaws are closed. On a closed-mouth croc, you can see only the fourth tooth of the lower jaw.

MATERIALS

Scissors
Paper-towel tube
Black, brown, and green markers
White craft glue
Cereal-box or shirt cardboard
Stapler

The Dino's Distant Cousins

CAUTION AHEAD! You are about to meet the world's largest modern-day reptiles: alligators and crocodiles. Crocs and 'gators are the only remaining group of *archosaurs,* or ruling reptiles ... the group to which dinosaurs belonged!

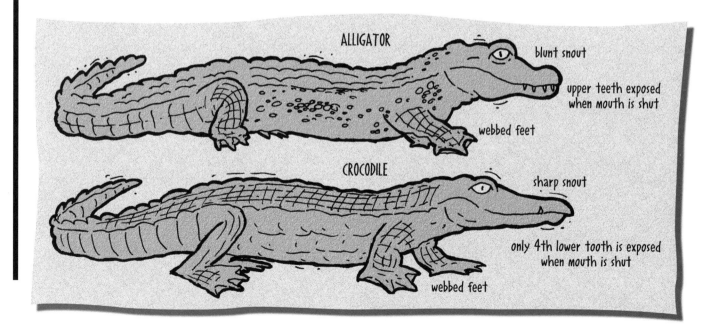

ALLIGATOR

blunt snout

upper teeth exposed when mouth is shut

webbed feet

CROCODILE

sharp snout

only 4th lower tooth is exposed when mouth is shut

webbed feet

Eyes

Legs

Lower jaw

LET'S DO IT!

1. Cut the paper tube in half lengthwise; then, cut out the alligator's body from the top half.

2. Cut out the alligator's lower jaw from the bottom half of the paper tube. Color with markers. Then, glue it to the upper jaw.

3. Cut out the alligator's eyes and legs from the cardboard. Staple the legs to the sides of the paper tube; then, bend the legs forward so the alligator lies flat.

4. Bend back the bottom edge of the alligator's eyes and glue to the top of the head. Draw the alligator's teeth so the upper teeth show (wouldn't want to confuse it with a croc!).

Living the Good Life!

SEE YA LATER, ALLIGATOR! Alligators and crocodiles have built-in snorkel-like gear (lucky, huh?). A fleshy valve in their throats keeps water out, and their eyes and nostrils are near the top of their heads, so they can breathe and see what is going on around them while their bodies are still underwater!

DENTAL HYGIENE! When a crocodile lies with its mouth open to cool off, a bird called a plover picks food from between its teeth. Yuck! But it works for this team: The plover gets a free dinner, and the croc gets free dental care (and no cavities!).

After you...

Green SEA TURTLE

CURATOR'S NOTES

GREEN SEA TURTLE

THEN: Mesozoic era, Triassic period, 250 to 205 mya

NOW: Kingdom: animals; Phylum: chordates (vertebrates); Class: reptiles

When you think of the word "turtle," what comes to your mind? A slow turtle plodding across the road? Get ready for a surprise: Sea turtles can propel themselves through the water at speeds of nearly 20 miles (32 km) an hour! Their broad flippers make them go fast — the same way you speed through the water with a set of flippers on your feet!

As the heavyweights of the turtle family, sea turtles can weigh hundreds of pounds (kg).

MATERIALS

Cooking oil

Medium-sized, ovenproof glass bowl

Salt dough*

Cookie sheet

Recycled aluminum foil

Green tempera paint, in a dish or lid

Paintbrush

Black marker

*Salt dough:
1½ cups/375 ml salt
4 cups/ 1 liter flour
1½ cups/375 ml water

LET'S DO IT!

1. Oil the outside of the inverted glass bowl. Press a ball of salt dough over the outside of the bowl to make a thin shell. Place the bowl with the dough shell on a cookie sheet.

2. Shape smaller balls of dough to be the turtle's head, flippers, and tail; then, press them into the dough shell. (Dampen the dough to join them more easily. A crumpled ball of foil helps prop up the turtle's head.)

3. Place the turtle — still on the glass bowl — in a 300°F (150°C) oven until the dough hardens but doesn't brown (about 30 minutes). Allow it to cool; then, carefully lift the turtle off the outside of the bowl.

4. Paint the turtle green. Allow to dry. Draw a black pattern on the sea turtle's shell to show the turtle's "plates."

A SAD TURTLE TALE

Baby turtles often are eaten on their trek to the ocean by crabs, herons, and gulls, but guess who their worst enemy is? Humans. That's right — us! Even though marine turtles are protected by law, they are still killed illegally to make exotic foods (like turtle soup), for their oil (to make cosmetics), and for their skin (all those turtleskin shoes, belts, and bags). It's a sad turtle tale, indeed!

To learn more about the sea turtle, visit the Conservation International website at:

www.conservation.org/

Home Again, Home Again

Every year, on spring and summer nights, female sea turtles come ashore onto sandy beaches to lay their eggs. But they don't choose just any beach: In an amazing feat of nature, female sea turtles return to the same beaches where they were once hatched!

You Are What You Eat!

The green sea turtle gets its name because of the color of the fat found in its flesh. How do you think that fat gets its color?

Answer: Sea grass, seaweed, and other green plants in shallow coastal waters make sea turtles green!

RATTLE! RATTLE! RATTLE!

... HISSSSSSSSS!

CURATOR'S NOTES

SNAKES

THEN: Mesozoic era, Jurassic period, 205 to 135 mya

NOW: Kingdom: animals; Phylum: chordates; Class: reptiles

Snakes inhabit all kinds of places — woods and open meadows, deserts and mountaintops, rivers and swamps, and even cities, trees, or the sea. Some are so small they can lie in the palm of your hand, while others, like the 30' (9 m) anaconda, are definitely BIG!

Many snakes are harmless to humans (they're more scared of you), but it's a good idea to keep your distance. Some, like the diamondback rattlesnake, use venom (a poisonous fluid) to kill their prey.

MATERIALS

Scissors

Tissue paper

Pipe cleaner

White craft glue

Scrap of red construction paper

Black, brown, and yellow markers

LET'S DO IT!

1. Cut tissue paper 3" (7.5 cm) wide and slightly longer than the pipe cleaner. Place the pipe cleaner in the center; then, fold tissue paper over the pipe cleaner a couple of times to make a 1" (2.5 cm) strip. Press the tissue paper down flat and glue it along its length.

2. Cut around one end of the strip for the snake's mouth. Cut out the snake's forked tongue from red construction paper and glue it inside the mouth. (On a real rattlesnake, that flickering forked tongue collects tiny particles from the air and the ground, then passes them to sensors in the roof of the mouth, so the snake can smell!)

3. Gently draw a snakeskin pattern. Add dark rings around the snake's tail for the rattles. Bend your finished snake into a curled position, ready to strike.

Quick Snake Takes!

SNAKE LEGS ◆ Snakes from lizards? That's right! Boa constrictors today have remnants of hind legs and a pelvis, evidence of evolution in action for sure!

OH, MY ACHING BACK ◆ Humans sometimes complain about their sore backs, but imagine if you had a backbone of as many as 400 bones instead of just 26 sections along your spine! A snake's body is all back (the backbone runs the length of the body), with strong ribs that expand so that the snake can swallow animals bigger than itself.

THIS RATTLE IS NO TOY! ◆ That special noisemaker on a rattlesnake's tail has a lot in common with you. The hollow rings of the rattle are formed from keratin — the same material that makes up human fingernails. When the tail is shaken, the rattles hit against one another, making a noise that sounds like insects buzzing, a warning to others to watch out!

DISCOVERY CORNER

Snake Slither

Even without arms or legs, snakes have no problem getting around. A snake can bunch up its body, then shoot forward, wriggle sideways over the ground, or crawl in a straight line.

TRY IT!

Have a snake race, slithering across the carpet or outside on the grass. Remember, no hands or legs allowed! Follow same general rules as on page 29 (crab walk race).

IF SOMEONE SAYS, "DINOSAUR" to you, you might have more than one picture come to mind — and you'd be absolutely right! Oh, yes, there was *T. rex,* to be sure, but there was also *Compsognathus,* a meat-eating dinosaur that wasn't even as big as a Thanksgiving turkey! Some dinos had "duck bills," while others had horns, or armor, or bony plates, or spiky "thumbs." There were big dinosaurs and small — more than 350 known kinds of dinosaurs, with new ones still being discovered today!

And then, it happened: All types and kinds and shapes of dinosaurs are thought to have become extinct, leaving only fossils to tell us their tales. (Or do dinosaurs live on in the image of our feathered friends today?)

So enter the HALL OF DINOSAURS to look, wonder, and listen to the stories about when dinosaurs ruled the earth!

Hey, Kids!
Don't miss the
DINO PARTY
at 2:00 P.M. today
in the GREAT HALL.
Sorry, but no grown-ups
allowed!

HALL OF
DINOSAURS

KNOW-IT-ALL
DINO QUIZ

1 The Mesozoic era, or the "middle life" of the earth, included three geologic periods. Do you know what they are? *(Hint: One has its name in the title of a very popular dinosaur book and movie.)*

2 What was one of the largest meat-eating dinosaurs that ever lived?

3 What was the smallest dinosaur?

4 What group were the largest dinosaurs part of?

5 What was the fastest dinosaur?

6 Which dinosaur had the smallest brain in relation to its body size?

7 Which dinosaur had the largest brain in relation to its size?

8 The movie *Jurassic Park* is based on a true story. True or false?

9 *Brontosaurus* was one of the largest dinosaurs. True or false?

10 All dinosaurs were carnivorous (ate meat). True or false?

11 Some dinosaurs lived for 200 years. True or false?

12 Baby dinosaurs were born live like human babies. True or false?

13 For about how many years did dinosaurs roam the earth? And how many years has it been since they were on earth?

14 All dinosaurs ruled the earth at the same time. True or false?

15 The duck-billed dinosaurs had the most teeth of any dinosaurs. True or false?

16 *Parasaurolophus,* a bony-headed dinosaur, used its head crest as a snorkel under water. True or false?

17 All dinosaurs dragged their tails on the ground, like modern lizards. True or false?

18 Dragons and dinosaurs are related. True or false?

19 The more years that separate us and the dinosaurs, the less likely we will ever learn what made them become extinct. True or false?

ANSWERS:

1. The three periods are the Triassic, the Jurassic, and the Cretaceous.

2. *Tyrannosaurus rex.*

3. The smallest adult dinosaur we know of was *Compsognathus* (205 to 135 mya), which was about as tall as a chicken but measured 3' (1 m) from head to tail.

4. The sauropods, such as *Seismosaurus* (205 to 135 mya; see page 76).

5. *Dromiceiomimus* (205 to 135 mya), one of the long-necked ornithomimosaurs (meaning "bird-mimic reptiles"). It had slim, powerful back legs for running swiftly, at speeds of about 43 mph (70 kph).

6. *Stegosaurus* (see page 70).

7. *Troodon,* a rare dino of Cretaceous times.

8. False. People and dinosaurs never lived on earth at the same time.

9. False. Actually, *Brontosaurus* never existed (see page 17)!

10. False. Many dinosaurs didn't eat any meat; they were herbivores (vegetarians).

11. True. Dinosaurs lived a long time!

12. False. Baby dinosaurs, like other reptiles, hatched from dino eggs. In fact, dinosaur embryos have been found fossilized in their eggs.

13. They roamed for 160 to 180 million years! And they have been extinct for about 65 million years. (That means those fossils we find are at least 65 million years old!)

14. False. Early dinosaurs died out and other dinosaurs took their place. The *Stegosaurus,* for example, became extinct long before the three-horned *Triceratops* (70 mya) came on the scene. The distance in time between *T. rex* and *Apatosaurus* (140 mya) is the same amount of time between *T. rex* and *your parents* — about 65 million years!

15. True. The dinosaurs called hadrosaurs ("bulky lizards," also known as duckbills) had hundreds of self-sharpening teeth in rows lining their jaws — about 960 teeth in all!

16. False. The hollow spaces in the head crest of *Parasaurolophus* acted like a trombone, allowing the dinosaurs to make very loud noises.

17. False. Some sauropods (the really big dinosaurs) probably did, but most dinosaurs had stiffened tails that they held off the ground.

18. False. Long ago, before people realized that there had been dinosaurs on earth, the dinosaur bones that were found were thought to be dragon bones. But dragons aren't real; they're only in our imaginations!

19. False. We are finding new dinosaurs at quite a rapid pace now, and with new technology, we may yet discover what became of them all.

WRONG!

Make a DINOSAUR

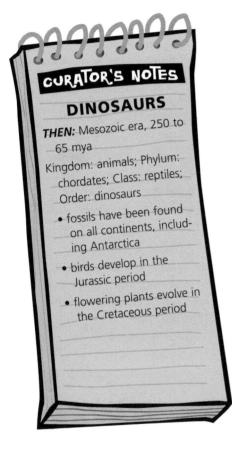

CURATOR'S NOTES

DINOSAURS

THEN: Mesozoic era, 250 to 65 mya

Kingdom: animals; Phylum: chordates; Class: reptiles; Order: dinosaurs

- fossils have been found on all continents, including Antarctica
- birds develop in the Jurassic period
- flowering plants evolve in the Cretaceous period

CLOTHESLINE TIME LINE

Dinosaurs took up so much time — about 160 million years — and there were so many of them (over 350 species) that they deserve a time line all their own!

Think of it this way: Humanlike creatures have lived on earth for less than 4 million years. In comparison, the dinosaurs lived on earth about 40 times as long! Here's a way to put them in order and chart their history through time. If you feel like hanging out (get it!), hang images of plants and other animals that lived at the same time.

1. Hang a long piece of rope or clothesline (about 40"/1 m long) across your room or down the hallway.

2. Write the word Triassic on a piece of notebook paper. Under Triassic write 250 mya. Then, on separate pieces of paper, write Jurassic, with 205 mya below it; write Cretaceous with 135 mya below that; write End of Dinos, 65 mya. (Need help? Ask a grown-up.)

3. Hang Triassic with a clothespin, paper clip, or tape all the way on the left. Move about 7" (17.5 cm) to the right of that and hang Jurassic; then, move 15" (37.5 cm) farther to the right and hang Cretaceous. Now, go 15" (37.5 cm) to the right again and hang End of Dinos.

4. As you go through the KIDS CAN! MUSEUM'S HALL OF DINOSAURS, add dinosaur images to your time line, in the time period that they lived on earth. Want to know when other dinosaurs lived? Look at pages 74 and 75, and at the books and Web sites listed on page 78. Then, add them to your clothesline time line. Some may overlap periods; some lived so far apart that it will seem hard to believe they were related! Have fun getting in a dinosaur frame of time!

A BRACHIOSAURUS skeleton Reconstruction

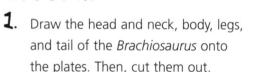

You know what a "reconstruction" is (see page 18). Well, you are going to be doing double duty here — building a reconstruction of one of the tallest dinosaurs and discovering what makes the BRACHIOSAURUS unique!

If BRACHIOSAURUS reached its enormously long neck upward in one of our cities today, it could have looked over the roof of a four-story building! (Howdy, folks!)

But let's see what it looked like underneath its skin.

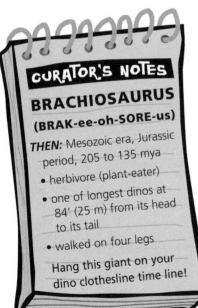

CURATOR'S NOTES

BRACHIOSAURUS

(BRAK-ee-oh-SORE-us)

THEN: Mesozoic era, Jurassic period, 205 to 135 mya

- herbivore (plant-eater)
- one of longest dinos at 84' (25 m) from its head to its tail
- walked on four legs

Hang this giant on your dino clothesline time line!

MATERIALS

Styrofoam plates, 2

Scissors

Ball-point pen

White craft glue

LET'S DO IT!

1. Draw the head and neck, body, legs, and tail of the *Brachiosaurus* onto the plates. Then, cut them out.

2. Cut out tiny U-shapes on the edges of the tail, neck, legs, and one side of the body, to look like a skeleton. Now, cut ribs into the opposite side of the body.

3. With ribs at the bottom, glue the head and neck onto one end of the body, and the tail onto the opposite end.

4. Cut two ½" (1 cm) slits in the rib-side of the body and insert the legs so the skeleton stands upright.

5. Now, stand back and admire your magnificent *Brachiosaurus* reconstruction!

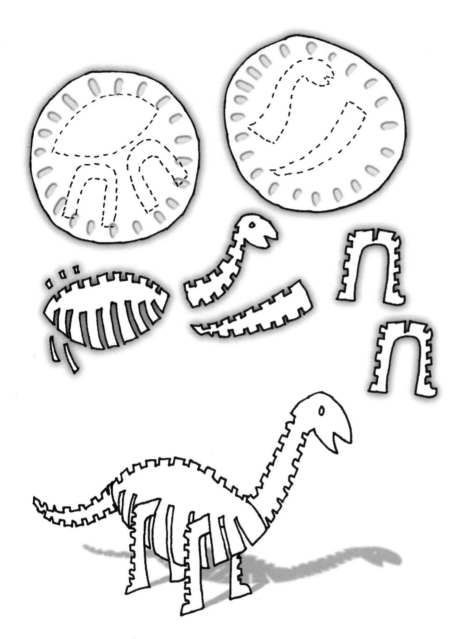

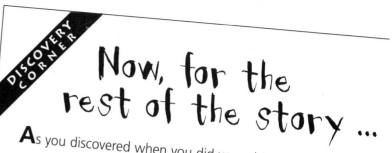
Now, for the rest of the story ...

As you discovered when you did your chicken bone reconstruction in the HALL OF HOW-TO TOOLS (page 16), bones don't tell the *whole* story.

TRY IT!

Draw a picture of your Brachiosaurus — skin, color, texture, details — using the "skeleton" you made as a model. Use your imagination; then, see what other scientists and artists believed this dinosaur looked like by looking at books about dinosaurs or by visiting dinosaur websites on the Internet (see page 78).

< HEADPHONES TO HISTORY >

During Dino Times

During dinosaur times, the world very gradually made remarkable changes. The continents began their long process of separating and then drifting toward the positions they have today. New types of flowers, trees, and animals developed. And, as the world changed, so did the dinosaurs!

In the Mesozoic era, the U.S. Midwest was like a dinosaur homeland. Of course, it didn't look like it does today: The Rocky Mountains were just hills. Some of the dinosaurs lived in evergreen forests, while others lived on open flood plains. The temperature was always warm, night and day, summer and winter.

Sounds real nice in dino land!

Bird-hipped

Lizard-hipped

Dinos Are HIP!

Yes, a dinosaur's hips, or *pelvis,* tells a lot about what that dino was like. Some dinosaurs, like *Brachiosaurus* and *Tyrannosaurus*, had hip bones that were wide apart, similar to a modern lizard's or crocodile's hips. Others, like *Stegosaurus*, had hip bones that were close together, like a bird's. All dinosaurs are part of either the *bird-hipped* or the *lizard-hipped* group — and both groups included dinosaurs that walked on two legs (like *T. rex*), or four legs (like *Brachiosaurus*).

A Dinosaur Is A . . . ?

What exactly is a dinosaur? Good question, especially since most scientists now believe that dinosaurs and birds are related (see page 86). You know some were big, some were ferocious, some ate plants, but what were they, really?

You know that dinosaurs were reptiles and share the reptile's characteristics: *vertebrate* (have backbones or spinal columns), *dry, scaly skin;* lay *eggs with shells;* and are *considered cold-blooded* (see page 31) ... sort of. You see, dinosaurs were different from other reptiles.

Take temperature, for one thing. Some dinosaurs, like *Dromaeosaurus,* were such fast, agile runners that scientists believe they may have been warm-blooded — acting more like a wolf (a mammal) than a reptile. Other dinosaurs, like *Stegosaurus*, used their bony plates to keep themselves warm. So were dinosaurs cold-blooded ... or maybe something in between cold and warm?

And dinosaur legs were different from other reptiles. Lucky for them! If you look at a more typical reptile like today's lizard, you will notice that its legs are held out from the sides of its body with the elbows and the knees bent. That's why its belly is so low: Its legs can't hold the weight any farther off the ground!

But a dinosaur's legs were tucked beneath its body, similar to the way your legs are positioned. That meant dinosaurs could walk and run much better than other reptiles. It also gave dinos the support they needed to grow larger ... and larger ... and larger! (If only they had a good pair of running shoes!)

A Stand-up STEGOSAURUS

Here's a dinosaur that wore its bones inside and out! STEGOSAURUS was covered with diamond-shaped plates (sheets of bone covered with skin) that jutted out down its neck and back. Some of the plates were as large as a small tabletop — 3' (1 m) across!

MATERIALS

Large white paper plates, 2

Scissors   Black marker

Paper tube   White craft glue

Tempera paints (you choose the colors)

LET'S DO IT!

1. Cut out the tail, legs, head, and spines of the *Stegosaurus* from paper plates. Sketch the face.

2. Cut a 3" (7.5-cm) slit in one end of the tube; glue and slide in the *Stegosaurus* body. Cut a ½" (1 cm) slit in the opposite end; glue and slide in the head.

3. Glue the legs onto the sides of the tube and the tail onto the body. Bend the feet to stand your *Stegosaurus* upright. Allow to dry.

4. Paint the *Stegosaurus* with tempera paint.

A Coat of Armor

The large, bony plates jutting out down *Stegosaurus*'s neck and back are called *scutes* (SKYOOTS). This armored protection may have made enemies think twice before biting into *Stegosaurus,* and it also may have helped the dinosaur keep warm or cool. What modern animals can you think of that have spines, plates, or tough shells? See below for six ideas to get you started!

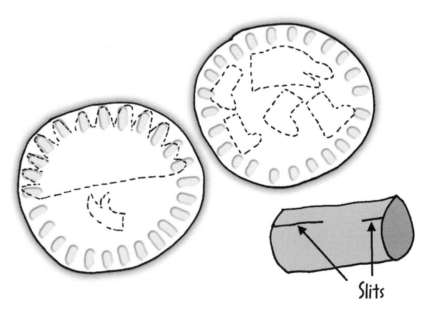

Slits

Answers: armadillos, turtles, lobsters, clams, mussels, oysters, for starters!

TYRANNOSAURUS REX!

Watch out! It's terrible TYRANNOSAURUS REX, one of the largest meat-eating dinosaurs that ever lived!

MATERIALS

Large white paper plates
Scissors
Black marker
Paper tube
White craft glue
Tempera paints

LET'S DO IT!

1. Cut out the large rear legs, short front legs ("forearms"), tail, and head from the paper plates. Then, draw on a *T. rex* face.

2. Cut a 3" (7.5 cm) slit in one end of the tube; glue and slide the tail in upright. Cut a ½" (1 cm) slit at the opposite end; glue and slide the head in.

3. Hold the tube at an angle, and glue the rear legs vertically onto the sides; then, glue on the shorter front legs. Allow to dry. Rest the tube on its edge and rear legs to stand your *T. rex* upright.

4. Paint the *T. rex* with tempera paints.

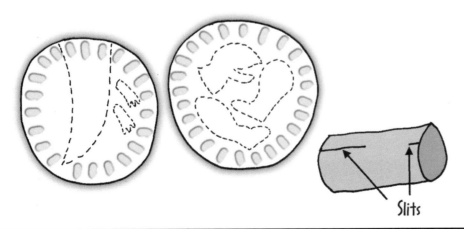

Slits

Neat Feet

*T*yrannosaurus rex walked on its two back feet, leaving sharply pointed birdlike prints with its three toes.

TRY IT!

Draw Tyrannosaurus feet on a recycled Styrofoam tray from fruits or vegetables. Cut them out. Dip the feet in a thin layer of tempera paint and press onto paper to make T. rex footprints. Continue the prints on blank newsprint to make your very own T. rex wrapping paper! Or, with permission, cut out a lot of feet and, using tape, have T. rex walk up your walls and across your ceiling!

The Dino Time Gallery

Step right into our dino time gallery and get up close and personal with some of your friends — dinos, reptiles, and early birds — from dinosaur times! Along with their portraits, notice the names of these reptiles translated from their Greek and Latin roots. TYRANNOSAURUS, for example, comes from Greek roots TYRANNOS and SAUROS, meaning "tyrant" + "lizard." Do you notice a match between names and physical characteristics?

Compsognathus
"elegant jaw" (Jurassic)

Pterodactylus
"winged fingers" (Jurassic)

Plateosaurus
"broad reptile" (Triassic)

Archaeopteryx
"primitive wing" (Jurassic)

Ceratosaurus
"horned face lizard" (Jurassic)

Stegosaurus
"roof lizard" (Jurassic)

Iguanodon
"iguana tooth" (Cretaceous)

Bananasaurus
"slippery peel" (Lunch, Dinner)

Big, Bigger, Biggest?

Though *Brachiosaurus* was big, fossils show that there were even taller and heavier dinosaurs. *Supersaurus* (SUE-per-SORE-us), found in Colorado in 1972, was 98' (30 m) long, head to tail — that's as long as about 20 kids your size, lined up head to toe! (Try that on the school playground some day.) Then five years later, a partial skeleton of an even bigger sauropod was discovered, and named *Ultrasaurus*.

One of the biggest dinosaurs on record is *Seismosaurus* or "earth shaker." It's estimated to be 130' to 160' (40 to 50 m) long head to tail, weighing in at about 51 tons. If placed on a modern-day football field, the *Seismosaurus*'s estimated length would reach from one end zone to the 50-yard line, and its weight would equal that of 46 VW Beetles!

Dinos in the Dirt

At the Dinosaur National Monument, the remains of nearly 100 Jurassic dinosaurs have been found. If you visit the Dinosaur Quarry Visitor Center near Jensen, Utah, you can watch paleontologists chip away at the ridge of rock that holds the fossilized bones! For more, check out the monument's website (www.nps.gov/dino/).

But as our knowledge increases with new finds, the records change. A new dinosaur discovered in southeastern Oklahoma in 1994 has been named *Sauroposeidon,* which means "earthquake god lizard." When it was first discovered, scientists thought the bones were the stumps of massive prehistoric trees! Its estimated weight is more than 60 tons, and it stood tall enough to look into a sixth-floor window! In fact, each neck bone is about 4' (1.5 m) tall — about as tall as you! Its neck was about a third longer than that of *Brachiosaurus.*

Let these creatures join your dinosaur time line!

BEEP!

A Dinosaur Named ...

Would you like to have a dinosaur named for you? It really could happen! When Christopher Wolfe was 7 years old, he found a dinosaur bone while fossil hunting in 1996 near the Arizona–New Mexico border with his parents. Christopher's dad, a paleontologist, found more dinosaur bones. They had stumbled upon an unknown species of horned dinosaur! Christopher's dad named the new species *Zuniceratops christopheri* ... after his son!

Extinct:
A species of animal that *no longer* exists on earth is *extinct.*

Evolve: When small changes over thousands or even millions of years cause one species of animal to gradually develop into a new animal species, we say that species has *evolved.*

WHAT HAPPENED TO THE DINOSAURS?

ECO-ALERT !

Dinosaurs became *extinct* (disappeared forever) long before people walked the earth, so scientists aren't sure why they all died. Some scientists believe they gradually became extinct, while others believe something catastrophic — like a series of giant asteroids crashing to earth — may have killed them.

Whatever happened, at the end of the Cretaceous period, about 65 million years ago, the dinosaurs, pterosaurs, and many other prehistoric creatures and plants disappeared — at least as we think of them back then. (New discoveries about how the dinosaurs lived, ate, kept warm, reproduced, and *may have evolved* continue to surprise and amaze us today!)

Check out the resources on page 78 for more on current dino finds and materials, and be sure to look in the HALL OF AMPHIBIANS AND REPTILES and the HALL OF BIRDS for some interesting thoughts relating to dinosaurs, too!

Dinos on the Internet!

Now that's pretty interesting — dinosaurs from millions of years ago are being talked about on the Internet which is new technology just happening now! Wow!

www.desertusa.com/mag98/dec/stories/dinosites.html

www.ucmp.berkeley.edu/diapsids/dinosaur.html

www.nmnh.si.edu/paleo/dino/

www.levins.com/dinosaur.html

www.wmnh.com

GROWLLLL...

DINO PAGE!!

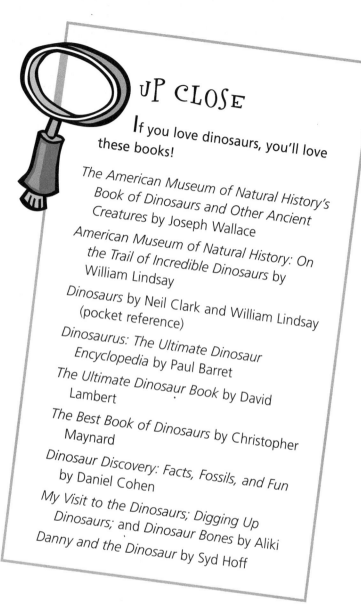

UP CLOSE

If you love dinosaurs, you'll love these books!

The American Museum of Natural History's Book of Dinosaurs and Other Ancient Creatures by Joseph Wallace

American Museum of Natural History: On the Trail of Incredible Dinosaurs by William Lindsay

Dinosaurs by Neil Clark and William Lindsay (pocket reference)

Dinosaurus: The Ultimate Dinosaur Encyclopedia by Paul Barret

The Ultimate Dinosaur Book by David Lambert

The Best Book of Dinosaurs by Christopher Maynard

Dinosaur Discovery: Facts, Fossils, and Fun by Daniel Cohen

My Visit to the Dinosaurs; Digging Up Dinosaurs; and *Dinosaur Bones* by Aliki

Danny and the Dinosaur by Syd Hoff

Party Time!

Now, let's head out to the GREAT HALL for that special dino party, which is just about to start!

KIDS CAN! Dino Party in the GREAT HALL

IT'S A DINOSAUR PARTY!

WHAT BETTER WAY TO CELEBRATE the Age of Dinosaurs than by having a party in honor of the mighty dinos themselves? Here in the GREAT HALL of the *KIDS CAN!* NATURAL HISTORY MUSEUM, the "kids only" dinosaur party is a tradition almost as old as the museum itself (which in dino terms is admittedly not very old at all). You'll find lots to do: T-shirts to paint, dinosaur-styled treats to eat, games to play — why even *T. rex* would be grinning!

So come along and join in the fun. We're very glad you are here!

GREAT HALL

Make a Dino T-shirt

Make a dinosaur T-shirt to wear as you roam the museum. Use the pictures from this book — er, museum — or draw your own, because anything goes. After all, it is your T-shirt!

MATERIALS

Dinosaur picture
Cardboard, from shirt or cereal box
Scissors
Cotton T-shirt, large-size, washed and dried
Clip-type clothespins
Graphite transfer paper (available from art or craft stores)
Pencil
Fabric paints or "puffy paints"
Paintbrush

LET'S DO IT!

1. Photocopy a dinosaur picture of your choice or draw your own freehand (adjust size of copy to front of shirt).

2. Cut the cardboard to fit inside the shirt. Stretch the T-shirt tightly across the cardboard; then, use the clothespins to secure it along the edges.

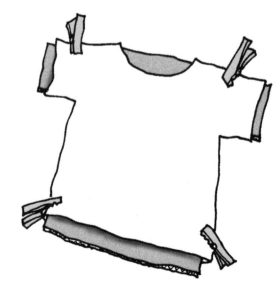

stegosaurus cake

3. Place the graphite transfer paper on the front of the shirt, graphite side down. Lay the dinosaur photocopy on top of the paper. Use the pencil to trace the outline of the dinosaur.

4. Paint the dinosaur with the fabric paint.

    NOTE: Some fabric paints come in squeeze tubes, eliminating the need for a brush.

5. Allow your T-shirt to dry completely before wearing it.

How about a special treat while your T-shirt art dries? As you munch on STEGOSAURUS cake, here's a question to ponder: If things like cakes were available, could T. REX have eaten a STEGOSAURUS cake? Why or why not?

INGREDIENTS

9" x 13" (22.5 x 32.5 cm) cake from cake mix (any flavor)

Sturdy cardboard, 12" x 24" piece (30 x 60 cm)

Aluminum foil

Green food coloring

White icing (1 can)

Wafer cookies

Serrated knife (for grown-up use only)

Candy for decorations (licorice, candy corn, jelly slices, etc.)

Answer: Well, they didn't live at the same time, as you know, but since *Stegosaurus* lived first, *T. rex* could have eaten a *Stegosaurus*-styled cake.

LET'S DO IT!

1. Allow cake to cool completely. Place it on the cardboard covered with foil.

2. Cut the cake in half, so there are two big squares. Cut across one square diagonally; cut around one end of the diagonal for a tail. Round off the top edges of the other square to make the body.

3. Place the tail against the body. Cut off two ends of the second diagonal. Round off ends to make legs; place against the underside of the body.

4. Cut out the head from the remaining cake section. Place the head up against the body.

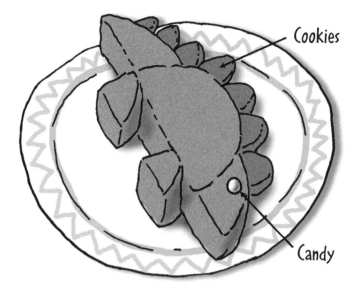

Cookies

Candy

5. Mix a few drops of green food color into the icing. Spread over the dinosaur.

6. Cut the wafer cookies on the diagonal and press them into the top of the dinosaur for scutes. Press the candy into the dinosaur for eyes and decorations. Serve with dino-egg ice cream!

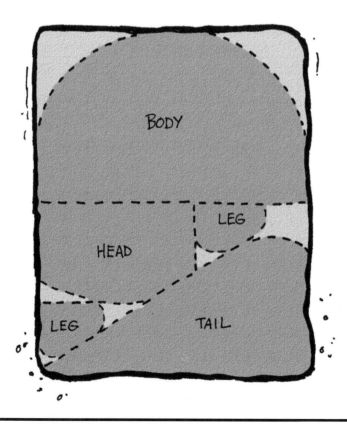

BODY

LEG

HEAD

LEG

TAIL

Dino-Egg Ice Cream

A few hours before the party, scoop ice cream and then roll individual scoops in colorful sprinkles. Place each scoop in a cupcake paper and freeze.

Make Your Own Dino Sock Puppet

Bring the Age of Dinosaurs to life by making your own dinosaur puppets. Then, imagine how dinosaurs might have communicated, and have some fun playing "dinosaur family" with some friends.

MATERIALS

Scissors
16-oz (500 ml) sturdy paper cup
White cotton athletic sock, or colored
Stapler
Green fabric paint (optional)
Scrap felt (assorted colors, including green)
Wiggly eyes
Fabric glue

LET'S DO IT!

1. Starting 1" (2.5 cm) below the rim of the paper cup, cut out an opening 1" (2.5 cm) wide. Cut down the side of the cup, across the bottom, and back up the opposite side, stopping 1" (2.5 cm) below the rim.

2. Slip the cup into the foot of the sock. Make a single cut through the sock, following the line of the cup's slit.

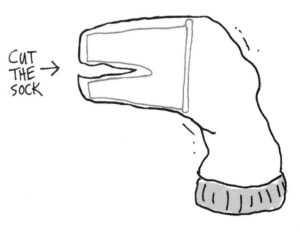

CUT THE SOCK →

83

3. Staple the cut edges of the sock to the top and bottom of the cup for the dino's mouth.

4. Use the fabric paint to paint the sock green (or use a colored sock instead).

5. Decide what you want your dinosaur to look like. Then, cut out the dino's legs and plates from felt scraps, and glue them onto the dino's body. Cut out eyes, nostrils, and teeth, and glue them on. Glue on wiggly eyes.

As the Clock Strikes . . .

Time to move along. You still have two more halls to visit — the HALL OF BIRDS and the HALL OF MAMMALS!

WITH THEIR BEAUTIFUL SONGS, bright feathers, and fragile wings, birds are a great source of pleasure — free for all who wish to enjoy! But what's *most* fascinating is that almost all of them can do something that we can't do, no matter how hard we try: *FLY!*

Luckily, you don't have to take wing to explore the amazing world of our feathered friends of the past and present. Find out what a "bird's-eye view" of life on earth is like in the *KIDS CAN!* MUSEUM'S HALL OF BIRDS, right now!

HALL OF
BIRDS

Is That a Dino That Just Flew By?

A silly question? Not at all. In fact, it's one of the most discussed topics of natural history today! Most paleontologists (see page 18) now believe that birds actually *descended* from the "killers" of the dino world: the meat-eating theropods that walked on their two rear feet. And new fossil discoveries are offering more evidence for a dino-bird link every day!

These scientists point out similarities — three-toed feet; wrists that swivel; lightweight skulls; wishbones, breastbones, and hollow bones — between modern birds, ancient birds, and the meat-eating, bipedal dinosaurs. They believe *Archaeopteryx* is a *transitional fossil* — something *in between* that shows the changes of evolution in progress. After all, dinosaurs were a type of reptile, and paleontologists know that what were once *scales* became the feathers of a bird. And new finds indicate that some of the theropod dinosaurs had feathers, too.

Because feathers are so delicate, they rarely turn up in fossils. So it could be that they were much more common than the fossil record actually reveals. *Velociraptor*s — those slashing, fast-running dinosaurs depicted in the book and movie *Jurassic Park* — actually had plumage and may even have been warm-blooded. Even the mighty *Tyrannosaurus rex*, the emperor of prehistoric meat-eaters, likely had downy feathers as a young hatchling!

News Flash!

The evidence is still coming in — and young paleontologists *your age* are helping to unravel the dino-bird mystery!

A baby dino named Bambi? Yes! And its bones (one of the most important fossil finds to be discovered in North America!) were unearthed by 14-year-old Wes Linster, who was hunting for fossils near Glacier National Park in Montana. He overturned a rock and saw a bone

with sharp, tiny black teeth on one side. It was the jaw of a baby birdlike raptor dinosaur that lived 72 million years ago — and he had uncovered the very first specimen!

The creature's roadrunner-like body had very long arms with hinged wrist joints that resembled clawed wings; thin, hairlike feathers; and a large brain (the skull is just slightly larger than a lightbulb) in relation to its body size — this dino was smart!

Wes nicknamed it "Bambiraptor" because it was small, like Bambi. But this creature definitely was not gentle — the retractable sickle-shaped claw on each foot would have been deadly to its prey. Scientists say *Bambiraptor* is one of the most convincing finds yet — right up there with the famous *Archaeopteryx* (see page 88) — that points to a link between dinos and birds.

You can check out the fossil, christened *Bambiraptor feinbergi,* online at Fossilwork Laboratories' site at www.bambiraptor.com or see the real thing at the Florida Institute of Paleontology at the Graves Museum near Ft. Lauderdale, Florida (www.gravesmuseum.org/).

Be a Paleontologist!

If dinosaurs really did *evolve* into birds in the evolutionary chain, then are dinos really *extinct?* (Remember, *extinct* means completely gone from earth, so that no new young are produced; *evolve* means very slow changes over many years until you look, behave, and adapt in a different way (see page 77). Are we at the end of the dino story ... or not? Hmm ... that's a tricky one. What do you think?

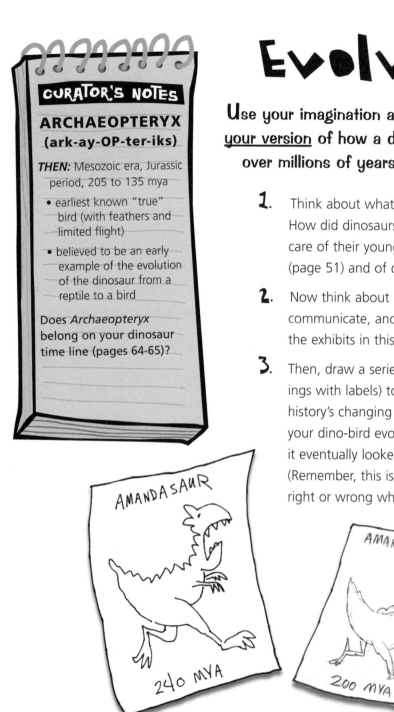

CURATOR'S NOTES

ARCHAEOPTERYX
(ark-ay-OP-ter-iks)

THEN: Mesozoic era, Jurassic period, 205 to 135 mya

- earliest known "true" bird (with feathers and limited flight)

- believed to be an early example of the evolution of the dinosaur from a reptile to a bird

Does *Archaeopteryx* belong on your dinosaur time line (pages 64-65)?

Evolving Art

Use your imagination and descriptive talents to show <u>your version</u> of how a dinosaur could have developed, over millions of years, into a bird you see today.

1. Think about what changes would have to take place? How did dinosaurs eat, move around, appear, and take care of their young? Look at descriptions of reptiles (page 51) and of dinosaurs (page 69).

2. Now think about how birds eat, move around, communicate, and take care of their young. (See the exhibits in this hall, pages 91–98.)

3. Then, draw a series of "scientific" pictures (drawings with labels) to illustrate your view of natural history's changing story. You may want to draw how your dino-bird evolved every 50 million years, until it eventually looked like a particular bird of today. (Remember, this is your interpretation — there's no right or wrong when it's in your mind's eye!)

AMANDASAUR

240 MYA

AMANDASAUR

200 MYA

AMANDASAUR

100 MYA

AMANDASAUR
65 MYA

AMANDASAUR
10 MYA

AMANDABIRD
TODAY

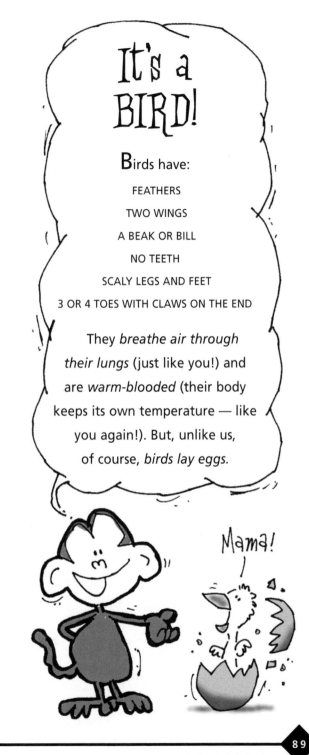

It's a BIRD!

Birds have:

FEATHERS

TWO WINGS

A BEAK OR BILL

NO TEETH

SCALY LEGS AND FEET

3 OR 4 TOES WITH CLAWS ON THE END

They *breathe air through their lungs* (just like you!) and are *warm-blooded* (their body keeps its own temperature — like you again!). But, unlike us, of course, *birds lay eggs.*

Mama!

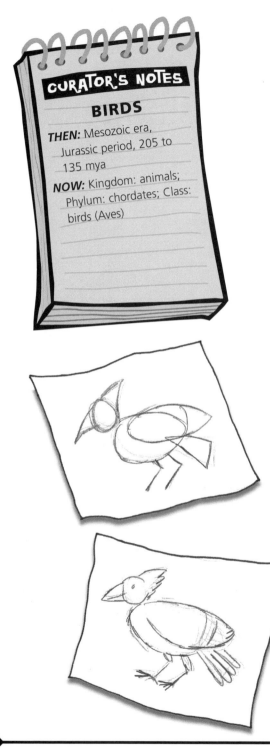

BIRDS

THEN: Mesozoic era, Jurassic period, 205 to 135 mya

NOW: Kingdom: animals; Phylum: chordates; Class: birds (Aves)

Quick-and-Easy BIRD ART

What is your favorite bird? A robin, an eagle, or perhaps your state bird? Sketch your favorite bird's portrait (you can find out the name of your state bird from your local tourist bureau or an almanac).

Drawing birds is as simple as 1, 2, 3. Just draw some shapes that you already know, in layers to "build" a bird.

LET'S DO IT!

1. Visualize your bird as a series of simple circles, triangles, and ovals. Look at some bird pictures with those shapes in mind to get you started. Begin with the large shapes of body, head, and wings. Lightly sketch the shapes in pencil or charcoal.

2. Then, still drawing in circles, triangles, and ovals, add shapes to represent beak, eyes, tail feathers, and any tufts or crests on the head.

3. Now, add more detail to your drawing to turn the shapes into the actual images. Smooth out points, blend lines together, and erase any stray lines.

4. Shade, color (colored pencils painted over with a bit of water work well), or paint your drawing. Try adding shading and details to make your bird appear three-dimensional.

Eat Like a Bird?

If your parents ever accused you of this, they probably meant that you didn't eat very much. But, the truth is, birds eat one-quarter to one-half of their weight in food each day!

TRY IT!

Figure out your bird weight by dividing your weight in half (your weight ÷ 2). Then, pile cans or boxes of food on your bathroom scale until you reach that number.

Bet your parents are glad that you don't really eat like a bird!

Come and Get It!

One way to be sure birds visit you regularly is to give them plenty to eat and drink.

TRY IT!

Keep it simple. When it comes to feeding birds, simpler is usually better.

◆ **Suspend a clean coffee can** *sideways* from a tree branch for a simple feeder. Just remove both the top and bottom from the can. Fill it with sunflower seeds (most birds love 'em), and toss some seed on the snow or ground.

◆ **Smear a pinecone with peanut butter**, dip it in birdseed, and hang it with string from a tree branch. You can even adorn an evergreen wreath with corn, pinecones, dried fruit, and nuts for a regular bird feast!

Don't forget the water. Birds like to have clean water to drink, and they appreciate a bit of water to dunk in to clean their feathers. If you're feeding birds in winter, check the water regularly to be sure it hasn't frozen over.

Make a PENGUIN

On land, penguins are downright comical, waddling side to side and dressed in their "tuxedos" of black and white. But in the water, it's another story! They speed along, using their strong wings as flippers, steering with their feet and tail. They're sleek and beautiful, at home in their habitat.

LET'S DO IT!

1. Cut out a penguin shape from one paper plate; then, cut out the wings, tail, and feet from the other. Slightly overlap the edges of the penguin shape and staple them together to make the body cylinder.

2. Paint your penguin's wings, tail, head, and back black. Paint the penguin's eyes and nose white. Allow the paint to dry.

3. Staple the wings to the top edge of the penguin's body, the feet to the bottom, and the tail to the back. Now, bend the feet forward, and press the head down to give your penguin its proper stance.

MATERIALS

Scissors

White paper plates, 2 large

Stapler

White and black tempera paint, in dishes or lids

Paintbrush

CURATOR'S NOTES

PENGUIN

THEN: Cenozoic era, Tertiary period, 65 mya

NOW: Kingdom: animals; Phylum: chordates; Class: birds

Grounded!

All birds have feathers; feathers help birds fly; but all birds don't fly. Why?

Sometimes it's a matter of size.

Ostriches, for example, have bodies so large that they are too heavy to fly. In evolutionary terms, the ostrich's wings are a *vestige*, a body part that used to be functional. At some point in the natural history of the ostrich, it traded the advantage of flight for the advantage of weight. (Why do you think that trade-off was made?)

But that doesn't slow them down at all! Instead, they *run*, using their powerful muscles to escape danger. The rhea, an extinct ostrichlike bird from South America, could sprint 31 mph (50 kph) — faster than a horse!

Sometimes it's a matter of evolutionary practicality.

Other birds, such as the colorful parrotlike kakapo of New Zealand, evolved on island homes where they had no need to fly. No need to fly? Well, if there were no predators on land and their food was on the land, why would they need to fly away?

And some birds, like penguins, take to the water, instead, for safety and for hunting. So they don't need to fly either.

Penguin Charades

Penguins make sounds to communicate, but they also use signals. If a penguin presses its feathers down when threatened, it's announcing, "I don't want to fight!" When it's time for dinner, penguin parents call loudly to their chicks (sound familiar?). And young penguins signal that they want to be fed by touching their parent's bill.

PLAY PENGUIN CHARADES. Have fun with nonverbal communication, penguin-style. How would *you* tell a group of friends "I'm losing feathers," "Come slide with me!" or "This fish is rotten!"? Make up your own penguin thoughts, and act them out. Your friends call out their interpretations of your actions until one person guesses what you're saying and becomes the next penguin.

AUK AUK
AUK

ERCH ERCH
ERCH ERCH...

UP CLOSE
And, for a funny glimpse of what life with penguins would be like away from their natural habitat, read *Mr. Popper's Penguins* by Richard and Florence Atwater.

An Eggs-ellent Idea

Most birds and penguins sit on their eggs in nests, but *emperor penguins* don't build nests to sit in. The female emperor penguin lays only one egg per mating season, and then she goes off to sea for about 65 days! (Thanks, Mom!) While Mom's at sea, the male penguin holds the egg with its feet to keep it off the cold ice. (Great job, Dad!) When you think about it, it makes you wonder how the emperor penguins ever had enough baby penguins hatch to keep their species alive! Just another one of the marvels of natural history's evolutionary tale!

TRY IT!

Hold a hard-cooked egg between your feet. Now try walking around the room. Imagine a penguin doing this in subzero temperatures with a fresh (and breakable) egg! (Those dads are very talented!)

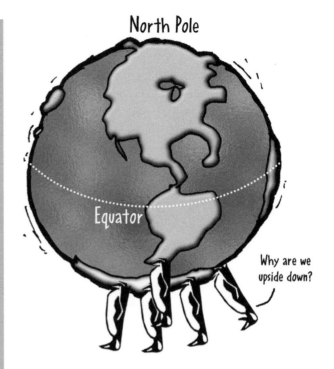

North Pole

Equator

Why are we upside down?

Where in the World?

Except for the penguins you see in zoos, most penguins live south of the equator — in the earth's *southern* hemisphere.

On a globe, find the equator, and then look for the continents of Australia and Antarctica. For a challenge, see if you can find the Galápagos Islands, off the west coast of South America. Some of the most famous finds of natural history and the process of evolution were discovered there!

Penguin Race

Have some fun balancing penguin-style in a relay using two kickballs (or similar-sized balls).

TO PLAY: Line up teams behind the starting line, with the first players placing the balls (the "penguin egg") between their ankles or knees. The first players run as fast as possible to the finish line and back, passing the "egg" to the next player. If a player drops the "egg," he or she must return to the starting line and begin again. The team that finishes the course first, wins.

CURATOR'S NOTES

FLAMINGO

THEN: Cenozoic era, Tertiary period, 30 mya

NOW: Kingdom: animals; Phylum: chordates; Class: birds

Food Coloring

The pale pink color of the flamingo's 25,000 feathers comes from a pigment in shrimps and other small creatures that the bird eats through its large bill. To feed, a flamingo dips its head upside down underwater and scoops it backward.

Bend your head down and scoop it backward, flamingo-fashion. Not so easy, is it?

— FLAMINGOS —
Pretty in Pink

The amazing color, flexible neck, and spindly legs of the flamingo make this waterbird really stand out! But when thinking about nature and natural history, it just boggles the mind to look at a flamingo and marvel at what an unusual-looking creature it is!

MATERIALS

Scissors

Cereal-box cardboard

Large white paper plate

Paper tube

Pink tempera paint, in dish or lid

Paintbrush

Popsicle stick

Transparent tape

White craft glue

Black marker

LET'S DO IT!

1. Cut out a flamingo's head, neck, and bent leg from the cardboard. Cut out wings from the paper plate. Paint them, plus the paper tube and the Popsicle stick, bright pink and let dry.

2. Cut a ½" (1 cm) slit in one end of the paper tube, and slide the flamingo's neck in place.

3. Cut two small parallel slits underneath the tube. Push a Popsicle stick into one slit and the bent leg into the other. Tape all parts in place.

4. Glue the flamingo's wings onto the sides of the tube. Draw on a black bill and eyes.

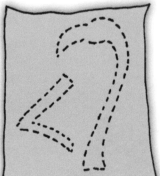

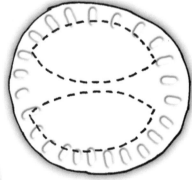

Slits

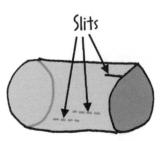

A Word on Waterbirds

As a waterbird, the flamingo's long legs allow it to wade into deep water, and its webbed feet work like paddles. Can you imagine a robin taking a dip in the deep end — never!

Think of a few other birds that live in or near the water. A duck will get you started. Now *you* think of five more that match this clue: The first letter of each bird's name helps spell the word "chess."

Take a Stand

You know, of course, that many birds gather in **flocks**. But some bird groups have special names. A gathering of flamingos, for instance, is called a **stand** (a perfect name for such long-legged birds). Geese gather in a **gaggle**, and chickens, a **clutch**. What about a **murder** of crows, a **mustering** of storks, a **paddling** of ducks, a **convocation** of eagles, a **band** of jays, a **tittering** of magpies, and an **exaltation** of larks? Wonderful words for these unique kinds of birds!

LOOK! A MURDER!

 **What's Next?** Well, if you have been following your KIDS CAN! MUSEUM map, you are probably ready to head to the HALL OF MAMMALS. So come on in — you just might see some familiar faces!

HERE'S A HALL that should make you feel right at home! I'm sure you can guess why: That's it — you'll come face-to-face with *you* in this very large hall! Did you know that there is no species of any phylum in the animal kingdom that is more highly evolved than the mammal that just happens to be you? It's true! So walk into the HALL OF MAMMALS, holding your head high and shoulders back in that famous two-footed stance of the most amazing creatures on earth — *Homo sapiens sapiens,* better known as humankind!

HALL OF MAMMALS

What Is a Mammal?

Bats and cats are both part of the same class — the *mammals* — in the animal kingdom. A pretty unlikely pair, right? One swoops in the sky; the other prowls and purrs with all four feet on the ground.

Let's take a closer look (taking notice of the creatures around us *today* is just another way to look at natural history). Though a bat may look more like a bird than a cat, can you think of anything bats and cats have in common? (Think about backbones, skin coverings, and whether the young are born alive.)

Cuddly cats are *warm-blooded*, *vertebrate* animals with *fur* (no scales or feathers here!). Same with bats — no feathers there, either! Both cats and bats like to keep their fur nice and clean by *grooming*, and they also *give birth to live young* (instead of laying eggs) and *nurse their babies*, feeding them milk produced by glands in the mother's body.

Sound familiar? Yes, humans are mammals, too! Take a closer look to discover other ways bats and cats (and *you)* are amazingly alike *and* wonderfully different!

CURATOR'S NOTES

MAMMALS

THEN: Mesozoic era, Triassic period, 250 to 205 mya
• first mammals appear
Cenozoic era, 65 mya to the present
• "Age of Mammals"

NOW: Kingdom: animals; Phylum: chordates; Class: mammals
• includes over 4,000 species

MAMMAL . . . or Not?

Now that you've met mammals, insects, birds, amphibians, arthropods, reptiles, and sea creatures, you pretty much know how to tell one from the other, right? Test your knowledge by playing Mammal ... or Not?

Mammal, mammal, mammal or not? I say a whale **is** a mammal.

ZACH

TO PLAY: This is most fun with two or more players. First player says, "Mammal, mammal, mammal or not? I say a snake (now say *is* or say *isn't*) a mammal." Any other player can answer: "I say a snake isn't a mammal because it has scales and no hair or fur!" (or give another true reason). If the player is correct, that player becomes the "Mammal-er." If the answer is incorrect, any player can correct it by saying the correct answer. If no one really knows or you think the Mammal-er is bluffing, you can challenge: Look it up in this book (see the index). The one who is right gets to be Mammal-er next. The faster the play, the better you get. Go for it!

Going BATTY

A bat's wings look paper-thin, but they're very strong, made of tough skin that stretches from their feet to the tips of their fingers. To fly, a bat flexes its wings up and down, pushing itself through the air.

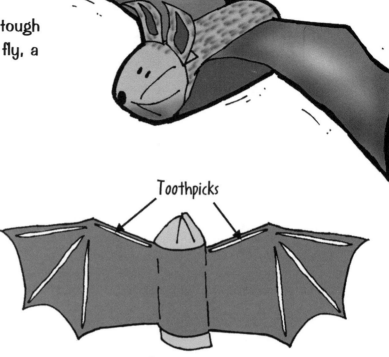

MATERIALS

Paper tube
Brown and black construction paper
Transparent tape
Scissors
Brown and black markers
White craft glue
Toothpicks

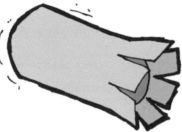

Toothpicks

Bottom view

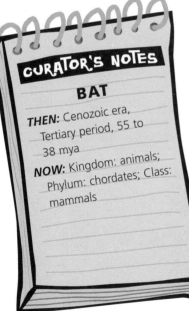

CURATOR'S NOTES

BAT

THEN: Cenozoic era, Tertiary period, 55 to 38 mya

NOW: Kingdom: animals; Phylum: chordates; Class: mammals

LET'S DO IT!

1. Cover the paper tube with a piece of brown construction paper, leaving about 1" (2.5 cm) hanging over one end of the tube. Tape along the bottom to hold.

2. Cut slits in the overhanging paper and tape together to make the bat's face. Draw on the eyes and nose; draw short fur on the body with markers.

3. Cut out the bat's ears from brown construction paper and glue onto the tube. Cut out the bat's wings from the black paper; glue onto the body.

4. Fasten toothpicks to the underside of the wings in the pattern shown. These are the bones of your bat's forearms, fingers, and thumb! See any resemblance to *your* fingers?

Hanging Around

Young bats, born hairless and blind, cling to their mother's fur with their toes. And when adult bats rest, they hang by their toes, upside down, too!

TRY IT!

Lie on a bed on your back, and hang your head and shoulders toward the floor. Do things look different (and feel funny) upside down, in bat-roosting position? To a bat, it's just normal behavior!

UP CLOSE

Read *Stellaluna* by Janell Cannon to find out how a baby bat learns to accept itself (and its batty way of doing things), amid a nest of baby birds.

Play Bat Tag

Bats depend on their sophisticated sonar and sense of hearing (called ECHOLOCATION) to find their way (and their supper) in the dark. To navigate, a bat squeaks, then listens as the sound bounces back. The echo tells the bat where it is and what else is nearby!

Use your sense of "location hearing" while playing tag, bat-fashion!

TO PLAY: Gather a few friends and go to an open field or big room to play. Blindfold one bat, "It." "It" listens to the other bats squeak and tries to tag them. None of the squeakers can move once the game starts, and they must continue squeaking throughout the game. Last squeaker tagged is "It" for the next round.

The Big Blue WHALE

What mammal is larger than a BRACHIOSAURUS and weighs as much as 5,000 kids all together? The blue whale! It's the largest animal alive today — on land, in the sea, or in the air.

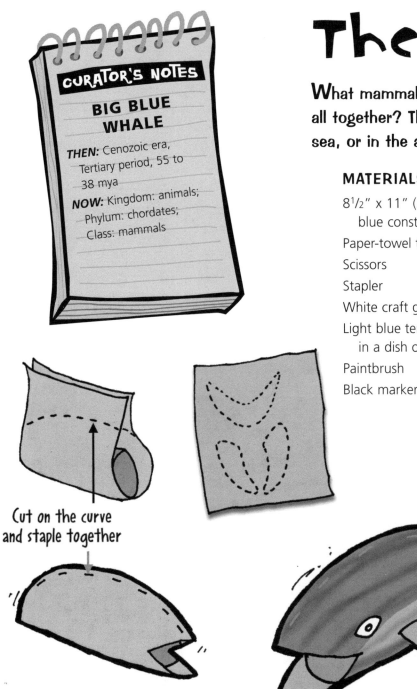

CURATOR'S NOTES

BIG BLUE WHALE

THEN: Cenozoic era, Tertiary period, 55 to 38 mya

NOW: Kingdom: animals; Phylum: chordates; Class: mammals

Cut on the curve and staple together

MATERIALS

8¹/₂" x 11" (21 x 27.5 cm) sheets of blue construction paper, 2

Paper-towel tube

Scissors

Stapler

White craft glue

Light blue tempera paint, in a dish or lid

Paintbrush

Black marker

LET'S DO IT!

1. Fold over one sheet of construction paper, holding the two sides together at the top. Slide the cardboard tube in the opening so that it rests at the fold.

2. Cut a curve across the top of the paper and staple together.

3. Cut a V-shape through the construction paper into one end of the tube to make the whale's mouth. Staple the paper around the mouth to the tube.

4. Cut out the whale's tail and fins from the second sheet of paper. Glue them in place: the tail in the opposite end of the tube and the fins onto the sides.

5. Brush the paint onto the bottom and sides of the whale and across the tail. Draw the whale's black eyes, mouth, and blowhole with the marker. Now, have a whale of a time with Big Blue!

I Brake for Whales

Sometimes, over millions of years, animals change so much that it is difficult to imagine that they evolved one to the other. That's the way it was with whales. As incredible as it sounds, whales were once animals that lived on *land!* The ancestor of the whale from way back when is believed to be the ancestor of today's hoofed plant-eaters — such as cows, horses, and rhinos — too! *Vestiges* (remaining features) of leg bones can actually still be found inside whales' huge, blubbery bodies!

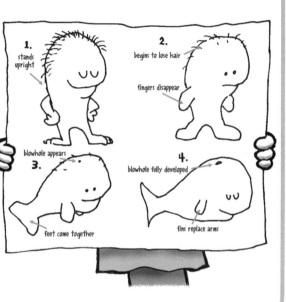

1. stands upright

2. begins to lose hair / fingers disappear

3. blowhole appears / feet come together

4. blowhole fully developed / fins replace arms

A WHALE of a Tale

You can write or draw your own!

TRY IT! Use your storytelling (or story-drawing) talents to describe, in your own "tall tale" picture-story, how a land animal could become a swimming whale. Think about what changes would have to occur, and make up a *fanciful* reason for why that might have happened. (Did the land-based whale get so mad it "blew its top" and had to cool off in the water?) Give your tall tale a title, such as "Why the Whale Has a Blowhole."

UP CLOSE

Rudyard Kipling, the author of *The Jungle Book*, had a great imagination about why animals changed. Read any of his stories, such as "How the Leopard Got His Spots" or "How the Elephant Got His Trunk" for some fun with natural history's tall tales!

GREAT SWIMMERS!

Is a whale a fish or a mammal? Is a shark a fish or a mammal? Now that you know the qualities of fish and the qualities of mammals, you can answer these questions. After all, some things just aren't as they appear.

If you go by appearances you might think both are fish: They both live and swim in the ocean.

But whales breathe through a blowhole at the top of their heads, so you'll occasionally see them coming to the water's surface. Sharks get oxygen from water filtered through their gills, so they can stay underwater. So where does that put you with the fish or mammal question for each?

Whales are warm-blooded; sharks are cold-blooded. (Keeping track of this?) And while all whales give birth to live young and nurse them as babies, some sharks lay eggs or even munch their own offspring for dinner! Ugh!

So what have you decided: fish or mammal, the same or different? See below for the answer!

Answer: Sharks are *fish*, and whales are *mammals*. For more on the fishiness of sharks, see page 31.

Saber-Toothed TIGER

When you think of a cat, you're most likely to imagine a pet that is soft and gentle, furry and cuddly. But lions and tigers are cats, too! The saber-toothed cat was a skillful hunter that lived during prehistoric times. (Its common name comes from its long 10"/25 cm-long teeth — shaped like daggers or swords.) The last of these fierce kitties were on earth at the same time as some of the earliest ancestors of humans.

MATERIALS

Scissors	Cereal-box cardboard
Brown construction paper	Tacky glue
Black and brown markers	White scrap paper
Paper tube	

LET'S DO IT!

1. Cut out the saber-toothed tiger's legs from the cardboard and trace onto brown paper. Cut out its tail, head, and legs from the brown paper. Glue the paper legs to the cardboard legs.

2. Use a black marker to draw the tiger's face. Cut out its teeth from the white paper and glue them onto the sides of the tiger's mouth.

3. Wrap the paper tube in brown paper and glue it to hold. Glue the tiger's legs to the sides of the tube. Glue its tail inside the tube. Glue its head over the tube's open end. Allow to dry.

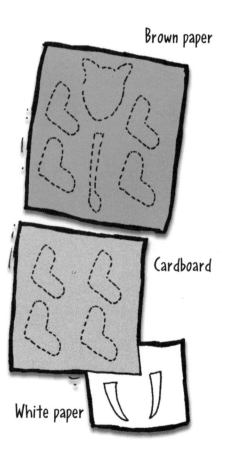

Brown paper

Cardboard

White paper

3-D Cat Mobile

Today, there are six "big cats." Can you name any of them? (Answers below.) Make a 3-D "cat family" mobile to show them off, along with a drawing of your favorite feline pet, if you like!

Cut through both pieces of paper

JAGUAR

MATERIALS

Paper

Pencil, scissors, markers, glue

Pipe cleaners (optional)

Cotton balls

Hole punch

Yarn or string

A stick or twig about 18" (45 cm) long

LET'S DO IT!

1. Fold six pieces of paper in half, and sketch the different cats (look in an encyclopedia or on the Internet for pictures of these wonderful creatures). Cut out around the outline, so that you have two pieces of paper for each cat; then, color them front and back and glue on pipe-cleaner whiskers.

2. Glue each cat together around the edges, leaving a small opening on one side. Stuff cotton balls inside and then glue closed.

3. Punch a hole in the top of each figure, thread with yarn, and then hang your three-dimensional cats from a wooden stick.

Answer: leopard, tiger, cougar, lion, jaguar, and cheetah

Make a woolly MAMMOTH

CURATOR'S NOTES

WOOLLY MAMMOTH

THEN: Cenozoic era, Tertiary period, about 2 mya

What do you put on when the weather gets cold outside? A woolly coat! Meet the massive elephantlike mammal from prehistoric times that had the woolliest coat of all — a perfect adaptation for life during the deep-freeze conditions of the ice ages.

MATERIALS

Large white paper plates, 2
Scissors
Paper tube
White craft glue
Brown tempera paint
Paintbrush
Brown and black markers

LET'S DO IT!

1. Cut out the mammoth's legs, tail, tusks, head, and trunk from the paper plates.

2. Cut a 3" (7.5 cm) slit in one end of the paper tube; slide in the mammoth's head. Cut a ½" (1 cm) slit in the opposite end; slide in the tail.

3. Glue the legs onto the sides of the tube and the tusks onto the sides of the trunk. Allow to dry. Bend the feet to stand the mammoth upright. Cut fringe around the head, legs, and tail.

4. Paint and draw features and fur on the mammoth's body and face.

MASTODON

IMPERIAL MAMMOTH

Mastodon or Mammoth?

Here are two very large creatures: Both belong to the elephant family; both have a long trunk and tusks. Many people think they are the same animal, but actually they lived at different times. Mastodons came on the scene first, about 30 mya, but woolly mammoths didn't appear until 2 mya — a blink of the eye in geologic time!

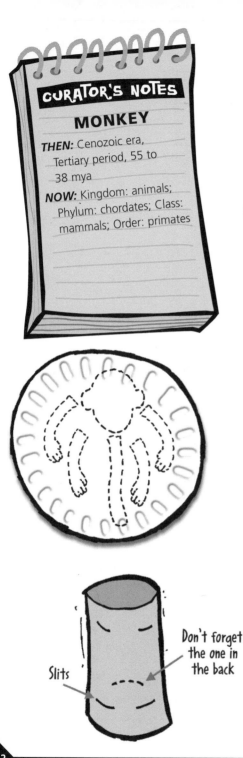

Slits

Don't forget the one in the back

MONKEY shines

An agile spider monkey can leap more than 30' (10 m) from branch to branch through the tall trees of the rainforest. As PRIMATES, monkeys are part of the highest order, or group, of mammals.

MATERIALS

Scissors
Large white paper plate
Black and brown markers
Paper tube
White craft glue
Brown tempera paint and sponge or paintbrush

LET'S DO IT!

1. Cut out the monkey's legs, arms, head, and tail from the paper plate. Draw on the monkey's face.

2. Cut four ½" (1 cm) horizontal slits in the front of the paper tube and one in the back.

3. Slide the monkey's arms and legs through the slits in front, and the tail through the slit in back; glue in place. Glue the monkey's face onto the tube.

4. Paint as desired. Now, swing your monkey through the trees!

Boy, he's a handsome devil!

Trapeze Act

The tall trees of the rainforest, where spider monkeys live, are the world's highest trapeze and tight-rope! But these monkeys don't give balancing a second thought. They have an amazing adaptation that makes them great acrobats: a strong, grasping (*prehensile*) tail that acts like a fifth hand and balancing pole. Spider monkeys almost never come down to the ground. Everything they need — leaves, nuts, seeds, fruits, and water — is up in the treetop canopy!

TRY IT!

Lay a line of string across the floor. Put one foot after the other, and walk across the string without stepping off. Next, try walking across the string holding a broomstick. Which way is easier to keep your balance?

Let Me See That!

Like spider monkeys, you have *binocular vision* — two eyes focused to give you the depth perception you need to judge distances as you walk, run, and skip. Binoculars operate the same way, focusing two eyes at the same time on a distant object.

TRY IT!

Looking through a pair of binoculars, cover one eye, then the other, and then look through with both eyes. How does your vision change?

Two-Footers!

Walk, run swiftly, stroll along, sashay or dance, or march with your feet way up high. Which way do you usually choose to get from here to there? Whatever your choice, you can bet it's on two legs and not four — just one of many traits that developed as modern-day humans took to the earth.

As a *primate,* you are part of the same group of mammals that includes apes, gorillas, chimpanzees, monkeys, and orangutans. Primates can be as different as a tiny, 2-ounce (50-g) mouse lemur and a 600-pound (300-kg) sumo wrestler! But as a *human,* you stand and walk upright — a perfect adaptation to your life on the ground.

CURATOR'S NOTES

AUSTRALOPITHECUS

THEN: Cenozoic era, Tertiary period, about 4 mya

NOW: Kingdom: animals; Phylum: chordates; Class: mammals; Order: primates; Family: hominids

Hello, Lucy!

Much of the information we know about early prehuman ancestors, called *hominids*, comes from the skeleton of a humanlike creature who lived more than 3 mya, nicknamed "Lucy" (much easier to say than her scientific name, *Australopithecus afarensis*). Lucy's bones show that she walked upright, stood about 3½' (1m) tall, and was about 20 years old when she died.

TRY IT!

Compare your height to Lucy's. Make a light mark in pencil on a piece of paper taped to a doorway, 3½' up from the floor, or make a notch in the bark of a tree outside. Then, ask a friend to mark your height. Are you taller or shorter than Lucy? How tall do you think you'll be when you're 20?

← Vickie
Age 9
4½ Ft.

→ Lucy
Age 20
3½ Ft.

← Tyler
Age 5
1½ Ft.

Good THINKING!

Walking upright wasn't the only trait that helped prehumans survive. They used their heads, too. As hominids evolved over millions of years into humans, their brains increased in size and they became smarter. All humans living today — including you! — are called *Homo sapiens sapiens* (meaning "double-wise man"). Take a bow — you are part of the brainiest species of all time!

And, like the humans who lived long ago, you use your skills to figure out how to survive ... and to express yourself in art!

Famous Finds

Imagine having your artwork on display for thousands of years! Yes, it can happen — it already has! Some of the oldest and most beautiful cave paintings and prehistoric rock artwork ever found were discovered in the Lacaux and Chauvet caves in France and the Altamira cave site in northern Spain. Scientists believe this art was made by the Cro-Magnons, who were *Homo sapiens* who lived 40,000 to 10,000 years ago. Quite an art show!

It's Art, Naturally!

No brushes, tempera paints, or crayons. No special papers and pastes. How did the earliest artists paint? The hunter-gatherer artists mixed charcoal and natural pigments with animal fat, water, vegetable juices — even blood! — and then applied the paint with their fingers, a stick, or a homemade "plant" brush to rocks, cave walls, and ceilings. They may have also used a hollow reed — sort of like a natural drinking straw — to give a "spray paint" effect.

LET'S DO IT!

1. Mix some hunter-gatherer paints from items found in nature. Collect mud, dirt, or pieces of bricks in different colors.

2. Use stones to grind them into a powder; then, mix with vegetable oil or water to make the paints.

3. For brighter colors, crush blueberries, strawberries, raspberries, or cherries with a spoon. Add a tablespoon or two of water or oil to the juice. Finger-paint a design on a rock, and try a spray-paint effect with a drinking straw.

All in the Family

Despite our many differences in how we look, what we wear, where we live, and how we do things, all *Homo sapiens* — all the people living on earth today, including you! — have a similar bone structure to all other *Homo sapiens*, including those who lived, say, 35,000 years ago. So a Cro-Magnon kid from way back when would look the same as a kid today. Cro-Magnon people even wore shirts with collars and cuffs and loved to wear jewelry!

CURATOR'S NOTES

MODERN HUMANS

THEN: Cenozoic era, Quaternary period, 10,000 years ago to present

NOW: Kingdom: animals; Phylum: chordates; Class: mammals; Order: primates; Family: hominids; Genus: Homo; Species: *sapiens*

SCHOOL BUS STOP

Make a "You" Cube

Show off your modern-day profile by making a 3-D portrait of yourself!

MATERIALS

Ruler and pencil
White construction paper
Scissors
Mirror
Markers, paints, or colored pencils
Square gift box
Wrapping paper
Tape

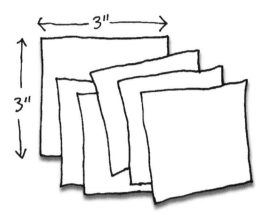

LET'S DO IT!

1. Using a ruler and pencil, measure six equal-sized squares, each about 3" x 3" (7.5 x 7.5 cm), on the construction paper. Cut them out.

2. Position a mirror in front of you; then, sketch your portrait, looking frequently into the mirror as you draw. Draw one view of your head on each side of five of the squares. Include the front view of your face (very important!), two side views, the back of your head, and the top (mostly hair!).

3. Cover a gift box with wrapping paper, and then tape each of the squares on a different side to make a lifelike cube. (The blank side goes on the bottom.)

You're looking soooo good!

Time to Go . . .

Well, we hope you've enjoyed your visit to the KIDS CAN! MUSEUM OF NATURAL HISTORY. And we hope you have a good idea of the characteristics of the different kinds of animals that inhabited the earth 570,000 years ago — all the way to today.

Every time you visit this museum you will learn something new about the *order of events* (remember the Before You/After You Time Line, page 6?), the *characteristics of groups* as you sort, group, and classify (see pages 2-5), and relationships found in the Biological Classification System and the Geologic Time Line, page 8.

For now, take your painted dino T-shirt and any other art projects you made, and imagine what life on earth might be like in the next 570 million years. Now, that is something to think about!

NATURAL HISTORY MUSEUMS

U.S. and Canada

THE ACADEMY OF NATURAL SCIENCES,
Philadelphia, PA

PHONE 215/299-1000
WEBSITE www.acnatsi.org/

AMERICAN MUSEUM OF NATURAL HISTORY, New York, NY

PHONE 212/769-5100
WEBSITE www.amnh.org/

CARNEGIE MUSEUM OF NATURAL HISTORY, Pittsburgh, PA

PHONE 412/622-1975
WEBSITE www.clpgh.org/cmnh/

CINCINNATI MUSEUM OF NATURAL HISTORY, Cincinnati, OH

PHONE 513/287-7000
WEBSITE www.cincinnatimuseum.org/

THE CLEVELAND MUSEUM OF NATURAL HISTORY, Cleveland, OH

PHONE 216/231-4600
WEBSITE www.cmnh.org/

DELAWARE MUSEUM OF NATURAL HISTORY AND SCIENCE, Wilmington, DE

PHONE 302/658-9111
WEBSITE www.delmnh.org/

DENVER MUSEUM OF NATURAL HISTORY, Denver, CO

PHONE 303/370-6357
WEBSITE www.dmnh.org/

FERNBANK MUSEUM OF NATURAL HISTORY, Atlanta, GA

PHONE 404/370-8077
WEBSITE www.fernbank.edu/museum/

THE FIELD MUSEUM OF NATURAL HISTORY, Chicago, IL

PHONE 312/922-9410
WEBSITE www.fmnh.org/

FLORIDA MUSEUM OF NATURAL HISTORY, Gainesville, FL

PHONE 352/846-2000
WEBSITE www.flmnh.ufl.edu/

THE GRAVES MUSEUM OF ARCHEOLOGY & NATURAL HISTORY, Dania Beach, FL

PHONE 954/925-7770
WEBSITE www.gravesmuseum.org/

HARVARD MUSEUM OF NATURAL HISTORY, MUSEUM OF COMPARATIVE ZOOLOGY, Harvard University, Cambridge, MA

PHONE 617/495-3045
WEBSITE www.hmnh.harvard.edu/

THE JAMES FORD BELL MUSEUM OF NATURAL HISTORY, Minneapolis, MN

PHONE 612/624-7083

National Museum of Natural History, Smithsonian Institution, Washington, DC

PHONE 202/357-2700
WEBSITE www.mnh.si.edu/

Natural History Museum of Los Angeles County, Los Angeles, CA

PHONE 213/763-DINO
WEBSITE www.nhm.org/

The Page Museum at the La Brea Tar Pits, Los Angeles, CA

PHONE 323/936-2230
WEBSITE www.tarpits.org/

Peabody Museum of Natural History at Yale University, New Haven, CT

PHONE 203/432-5050
WEBSITE www.peabody.yale.edu/

Pioneer Trails Regional Museum, Bowman, ND

PHONE 701/523-3600
WEBSITE www.ptrm.org/

Provincial Museum of Alberta, Edmonton, AB, Canada

WEBSITE www.pma.edmonton.ab.ca/

Royal British Columbia Museum, Victoria, BC, Canada

WEBSITE rbcm1.rbcm.gov.bc.ca/

Royal Ontario Museum, Toronto, ON, Canada

WEBSITE www.rom.on.ca/

San Diego Natural History Museum, San Diego, CA

PHONE 619/232-3821
WEBSITE www.sdnhm.org/

Schiele Museum of Natural History, Gastonia, NC

PHONE 704/866-6900
WEBSITE www.scheilemuseum.org/

Utah Museum of Natural History, Salt Lake City, UT

PHONE 801/581-4303
WEBSITE www.umnh.utah.edu/

World Museums

Musèe National d'Historie, Luxembourg

Musèum National d'Historie Naturelle, Paris, France

Natural History Museum, Berne, Switzerland

The Natural History Museum, London, England

WEBSITE www.nhm.ac.uk/

INDEX

Linster, Wes, 87
lizards, 51, 69
lobsters, 5, 21, 27, 71
"Lucy" (*Australopithecus afarensis*), 115

M

mammals, 5, 21, 99–120
   apes and monkeys, 5, 112–114
   armadillos, 71
   Australopithecus afarensis ("Lucy"), 115
   bats, 5, 100, 102–104
   cats, 5, 100, 108
   characteristics of, 100, 107
   classification of, 5
   humans, 5, 32, 57, 99, 114–119
   mastodons, 111
   saber-toothed tigers, 108
   whales, 4, 21, 105–107
   woolly mammoths, 13, 110–111
Marsh, O. C., 17
mastodons, 111
McIntosh, Jack, 17
Mesozoic era, 7–8, 10, 41, 48, 52–53, 56, 59, 62, 64, 66, 68, 70, 72, 88, 90, 101
mollusks, 5, 21–22, 25–26, 71
monarch butterfly caterpillar, 42–43
monkeys, 5, 112–114
Montana, 87
museum artists, 18
mussels, 21, 25, 71
mya (defined), 11, 20

N

newts, 5

O

octopuses, 25
Ordovician period, 8, 25, 27
organizing information, 2–7
ornithomimosaurs, 62–63
ostriches and rhea, 93
oysters, 5, 25, 71

P

paleo- (defined), 9
paleontology and paleontologists, 17–18
Paleozoic era, 7–9, 20, 22-23, 25, 27, 30, 35, 37, 48, 51. *See also* Cambrian period; Carboniferous period; Devonian period; Ordovician period; Permian period; Silurian period
Parasaurolophus, 62–63
penguins, 92–95
Permian period, 8, 37
plants, 32, 40–42, 64
Plateosaurus, 74
Plesiosaurus, 52
pliosaurs, 52
plover, 55
pollination, 41
prehistoric art, 116–117
primates, 112–119
Pteranodon, 53
Pterodactylus, 52, 74
pterosaurs, 52–53

Q

Quaternary period, 117–118

R

radial symmetry (defined), 23
rattlesnakes, 59–60
rays, 5, 21–22
reading suggestions
   dinosaur books, 78
   Frog and Toad Are Friends (Lobel), 50
   The Jungle Book (Kipling), 106
   Monarch Magic! (Rosenblatt), 44
   Mr. Popper's Penguins (Atwater), 94
   Stellaluna (Cannon), 103
   A Walk on the Great Barrier Reef (Arnold), 21
recipes
   Dino-Egg Ice Cream, 82
   edible "insects-in-amber," 36
   hunter-gatherer paints, 117
   salt dough, 20, 56
   Stegosaurus Cake, 81–82
reconstructionists, 18
regeneration, 24
reptiles, 47, 51–60. *See also* dinosaurs
   alligators, 5, 54
   archosaurs, 54–55
   characteristics of, 51, 69
   classification of, 5
   crocodiles, 51, 54–55
   Icthyosaurus, 52
   lizards, 51, 69
   Plesiosaurus, 52
   pliosaurs, 52
   Pteranodon, 53
   Pterodactylus, 52
   pterosaurs, 52–53
   snakes, 5, 51, 59–60
   turtles, 5, 51, 56–58, 71

MORE GOOD BOOKS

from WILLIAMSON PUBLISHING

Williamson books are available from your bookseller or directly from Williamson Publishing. Please see the last page for ordering information or to visit our website. Thank you.

MORE WILLIAMSON BOOKS BY JUDY PRESS!

AROUND-THE-WORLD ART & ACTIVITIES
Visiting the 7 Continents through Craft Fun

Ages 3 to 7, 144 pages, fully illustrated, trade paper, 10 x 8, $12.95.
A Williamson *Little Hands*® Book

ARTSTARTS FOR LITTLE HANDS
Fun & Discoveries for 3- to 7-Year-Olds

144 pages, fully illustrated, trade paper, 10 x 8, $12.95.
A Williamson *Little Hands*® Book

☆ *Parent's Guide Award*
ALPHABET ART
With A to Z Animal Art & Fingerplays

Ages 2 to 6, 144 pages, fully illustrated, trade paper, 10 x 8, $12.95.
A Williamson *Little Hands*® Book

☆ *Real Life Award*
☆ *Children's Book-of-the-Month Club Main Selection*
THE LITTLE HANDS ART BOOK
Exploring Arts & Crafts with 2- to 6-Year-Olds

160 pages, fully illustrated, trade paper, 10 x 8, $12.95.
A Williamson *Little Hands*® Book

☆ *Parent's Choice Approved*
THE LITTLE HANDS BIG FUN CRAFT BOOK
Creative Fun for 2- to 6-Year-Olds

144 pages, fully illustrated, trade paper, 10 x 8, $12.95.
A Williamson *Little Hands*® Book

☆ *Early Childhood News Directors' Choice Award*
☆ *Real Life Award*
VROOM! VROOM!
Making 'dozers, 'copters, trucks & more

Ages 4 to 10, 160 pages, fully illustrated, trade paper, 11 x 8¹/₂, $12.95
A Williamson *Kids Can!*® Book

WILLIAMSON'S *KIDS CAN!*® BOOKS . . .

Where all kids can soar!

The following *Kids Can!*® books for children ages 5 to 13 are each 144 to 178 pages, fully illustrated, trade paper, 11 x 8¹/₂, $12.95 US.

WILLIAMSON'S *KIDS CAN!*® BOOKS
Art & Crafts

☆ *American Bookseller Pick of the Lists*
☆ *Dr. Toy Best Vacation Product*
KIDS' CRAZY ART CONCOCTIONS
50 Mysterious Mixtures for Art & Craft Fun
by Jill Frankel Hauser

☆ *Parents' Choice Gold Award*
☆ *American Bookseller Pick of the Lists*
☆ *Oppenheim Toy Portfolio Best Book Award*
THE KIDS' MULTICULTURAL ART BOOK
Art & Craft Experiences from Around the World
by Alexandra M. Terzian

KIDS' ART WORKS!
Creating with Color, Design, Texture & More
by Sandi Henry

☆ *Teachers' Choice Award*
☆ *Parent's Guide Children's Media Award*
☆ *Dr. Toy Best Vacation Product*
CUT–PAPER PLAY!
Dazzling Creations from Construction Paper
by Sandi Henry

☆ *Parents' Choice Approved*
☆ *Parent's Guide Children's Media Award*
MAKING COOL CRAFTS & AWESOME ART!
A Kids' Treasure Trove of Fabulous Fun
by Roberta Gould

☆ *American Bookseller Pick of the Lists*
☆ *Parents' Choice Recommended*
ADVENTURES IN ART
Art & Craft Experiences for 8- to 13-Year-Olds
by Susan Milord

☆ *Parents' Choice Approved*
KIDS CREATE!
Art & Craft Experiences for 3- to 9-Year-Olds
by Laurie Carlson

☆ *American Bookseller Pick of the Lists*
☆ *Oppenheim Toy Portfolio Best Book Award*
☆ *Skipping Stones Nature & Ecology Honor Award*
ECOART!
Earth-Friendly Art & Craft Experiences for 3- to 9-Year-Olds
by Laurie Carlson

☆ *Parent's Guide Children's Media Award*
☆ *Benjamin Franklin Best Education/ Teaching Book Award*
HAND–PRINT ANIMAL ART
by Carolyn Carreiro
full color, $14.95

WILLIAMSON'S *KIDS CAN!*® BOOKS
Science

THE KIDS' BOOK OF WEATHER FORECASTING
Build a Weather Station, "Read" the Sky & Make Predictions!
with meteorologist Mark Breen & Kathleen Friestad

☆ *American Bookseller Pick of the Lists*
☆ *Parents' Choice Honor Award*
GIZMOS & GADGETS
Creating Science Contraptions that Work (& Knowing Why)
by Jill Frankel Hauser

☆ *American Bookseller Pick of the Lists*
☆ *Oppenheim Toy Portfolio Best Book Award*
☆ *Teachers' Choice Award*
☆ *Benjamin Franklin Best Juvenile Nonfiction
   Award*

SUPER SCIENCE CONCOCTIONS
50 Mysterious Mixtures for Fabulous Fun

by Jill Frankel Hauser

☆ *American Bookseller Pick of the Lists*
☆ *Oppenheim Toy Portfolio Best Book Award*
☆ *Benjamin Franklin Best Education/
   Teaching Book Award*

THE KIDS' SCIENCE BOOK
Creative Experiences for Hands-On Fun

by Robert Hirschfeld & Nancy White

☆ *Parents' Choice Gold Award*
☆ *Dr. Toy Best Vacation Product*

THE KIDS' NATURE BOOK
365 Indoor/Outdoor Activities and Experiences

by Susan Milord

THE KIDS' WILDLIFE BOOK
Exploring Animal Worlds through
Indoor/Outdoor Crafts & Experiences

by Warner Shedd

☆ *American Bookseller Pick of the Lists*
☆ *Oppenheim Toy Portfolio Best Book Award*
☆ *Parents' Choice Approved*
☆ *Parent's Guide Children's Media Award*

SUMMER FUN!
60 Activities for a Kid-Perfect Summer

by Susan Williamson

☆ *Selection of Book-of-the-Month;
   Scholastic Book Clubs*

KIDS COOK!
Fabulous Food for the Whole Family

by Sarah Williamson & Zachary Williamson

☆ *Benjamin Franklin Best Multicultural
   Book Award*
☆ *Parents' Choice Approved*
☆ *Skipping Stones Multicultural Honor Award*

THE KIDS' MULTICULTURAL COOKBOOK
Food & Fun Around the World

by Deanna F. Cook

☆ *Parents' Choice Approved*
☆ *Parent's Guide Children's Media Award*

BOREDOM BUSTERS!
The Curious Kids' Activity Book

by Avery Hart and Paul Mantell

☆ *Parents' Choice Gold Award*
☆ *Benjamin Franklin Best Juvenile Nonfiction
   Award*

KIDS MAKE MUSIC!
Clapping and Tapping from Bach to Rock

by Avery Hart and Paul Mantell

HANDS AROUND THE WORLD
365 Creative Ways to Build Cultural Awareness
& Global Respect

by Susan Milord

☆ *Dr. Toy Best Vacation Product*
☆ *Parents' Choice Approved*

KIDS GARDEN!
The Anytime, Anyplace Guide to Sowing
& Growing Fun

by Avery Hart and Paul Mantell

☆ *Parents Magazine Parents' Pick*

KIDS LEARN AMERICA!
Bringing Geography to Life with People, Places,
& History

by Patricia Gordon & Reed C. Snow

☆ *Children's Book-of-the-Month Club Selection*

KIDS' COMPUTER CREATIONS
Using Your Computer for Art & Craft Fun

by Carol Sabbeth

Visit Our Website!

To see what's new at Williamson, learn about our *Little Hands®* books for 2– to 6–year–olds, and learn more about specific books, visit our website at:

www.williamsonbooks.com

To Order Books:

You'll find Williamson books at your favorite bookseller, or order directly from Williamson Publishing. We accept Visa and MasterCard (please include the number and expiration date).

TOLL-FREE PHONE ORDERS with credit cards: 1-800-234-8791

Or, **SEND A CHECK WITH YOUR ORDER** to:

WILLIAMSON PUBLISHING COMPANY

P.O. Box 185   Charlotte, Vermont 05445

E-MAIL ORDERS with credit cards: order@williamsonbooks.com

CATALOG REQUEST: mail, phone, or e-mail

Please add $3.20 for postage for one book plus 50 cents for each additional book.

Satisfaction is guaranteed or full refund.

Prices may be slightly higher when purchased in Canada.

Kids Can!®, *Little Hands*®, *Kaleidoscope Kids*®, and *Tales Alive!*® are registered trademarks of Williamson Publishing. *Good Times!*™ and *Quick Starts*™ *for Kids!* are trademarks of Williamson Publishing.